ABOUT KANE: The Playwright and the Work

Graham Saunders lectures in Theatre Studies at the University of Reading. He is author of *Love me or Kill me: Sarah Kane and the Theatre of Extremes* (Manchester: MUP, 2002), *Patrick Marber's Closer* (Continuum, 2008) and co-editor of *Cool Britannia: Political Theatre in the 1990s* (Palgrave, 2008). He is also a series editor for Continuum's *Modern Theatre Guides*. He has contributed articles on contemporary British and Irish drama to journals including *Modern Drama*, *Journal of Beckett Studies*, *Contemporary Theatre Review*, *Theatre Research International*, *New Theatre Quarterly* and *Studies in Theatre and Performance*.

Series Editor: Emeritus Professor Philip Roberts was Professor of Drama and Theatre Studies, and Director of the Workshop Theatre in the University of Leeds from 1998 to 2004. Educated at Oxford and Edinburgh, he held posts in the Universities of Newcastle and Sheffield before arriving in Leeds. His publications include: *Absalom and Achitophel and Other Poems* (Collins, 1973), *The Diary of Sir David Hamilton, 1709–1714* (Clarendon Press, 1975), *Edward Bond: A Companion to the Plays* (Theatre Quarterly Pubs., 1978), *Edward Bond: Theatre Poems and Songs* (Methuen, 1978), *Bond on File* (Methuen, 1985), *The Royal Court Theatre, 1965–1972* (Routledge, 1986), *Plays without Wires* (Sheffield Academic Press, 1989), *The Royal Court Theatre and the Modern Stage* (CUP, 1999), *Taking Stock: The Theatre of Max Stafford-Clark* (with Max Stafford-Clark) (Nick Hern Books, 2007), *About Churchill: The Playwright and the Work* (Faber and Faber, 2008).

Series Editor: Richard Boon is Professor of Drama and Director of Research at the University of Hull. He is the author of a number of studies of modern British political theatre, including *Brenton the Playwright* (Methuen, 1991), and is co-editor of *Theatre Matters: Performance and Culture on the World Stage* (CUP, 1998). He is also author of *About Hare: The Playwright and the Work* (Faber and Faber, 2003) and editor of *The Cambridge Companion to David Hare* (CUP, 2007).

ABOUT KANE
The Playwright and the Work

Graham Saunders

faber and faber

First published in 2009
by Faber and Faber Ltd
Bloomsbury House,
74–77 Great Russell Street,
London WC1B 3DA

Typeset by Wordsense Limited
Printed and bound by CPI Group (UK) Ltd., Croydon, CR0 4YY

The right of Graham Saunders to be identified as author of this work
has been asserted in accordance with Section 77 of the Copyright,
Designs and Patents Act 1988

A CIP record for this book
is available from the British Library

ISBN 978-0-571-22961-1

2 4 6 8 10 9 7 5 3

For Joe and Ella Ballantyne

Contents

Editors' Note

There are few theatre books which allow direct access to the playwright or to those whose business it is to translate the script into performance. These volumes aim to deal directly with the writer and with other theatre workers (directors, actors, designers and similar figures) who realise in performance the words on the page.

The subjects of the series are some of the most important and influential writers from post-war British and Irish theatre. Each volume contains an introduction which sets the work of the writer in the relevant historical, social and political context, followed by a digest of interviews and other material which allows the writer, in his own words, to trace his evolution as a dramatist. Some of this material is new, as is, in large part, the material especially gathered from the writers' collaborators and fellow theatre workers. The volumes conclude with annotated bibliographies. In all, we hope the books will provide a wealth of information in accessible form, and real insight into some of the major dramatists of our day.

Abbreviations

AS: Aleks Sierz, *In-Yer-Face Theatre: British Drama Today* (London: Faber, 2001)

GS: Graham Saunders, 'Love me or Kill Me': *Sarah Kane and the Theatre of Extremes* (Manchester: University of Manchester Press, 2002)

All other references are given in the endnotes for each chapter.

A Note on the Text

All quotations from the plays of Sarah Kane, unless otherwise stated, are from *Sarah Kane: Complete Plays* (London, 2001).

A Chronology of Sarah Kane's Work and Significant Productions

For a comprehensive list of professional and amateur productions since 2001, see www.iainfisher.com.

1995	18 January: *Blasted*, Royal Court Theatre Upstairs, London.
–	October: *Skin* screened at the London Film Festival.
1996	15 May: *Phaedra's Love*, Gate Theatre, London.
1997	17 June: *Skin* screened on British terrestrial television (Channel 4) at 11.35 p.m.
1998	30 April: *Cleansed*, Royal Court Theatre Downstairs (temporarily located at the Duke of York's Theatre), London.
–	4 August: *Crave* previews at the Chelsea Centre, London.
–	13 August: *Crave* performed at the Traverse Theatre, Edinburgh.
–	8 September: *Crave* transfers to the Royal Court Theatre Upstairs (temporarily located at the Ambassadors Theatre), London. The production also toured to Germany, Dublin, Copenhagen, Denmark and the Netherlands.
–	12 December: German premiere of *Cleansed* at Hamburg Kammerspiele, directed by Peter Zadek.
2000	23 March: German premiere of *Crave* at Schaubühne am Lehniner Platz, Berlin; director Thomas Ostermeier.
–	23 June: *4.48 Psychosis*, Royal Court Theatre Upstairs, London.

–	October: Intercity Italian Festival at Sesto Fiorentino devoted to Sarah Kane. Revivals of Barbara Nativi's production of *Blasted* as well as *Crave*.
–	November–December: *Crave*, Axis Theatre Company, New York. First American production of the play. Deborah Harry (singer from beat group Blondie) played the role of M.
2001	April–June: Sarah Kane Season at the Royal Court. New production of *Blasted* directed by James Macdonald; revival of the 2000 production of *4.48 Psychosis* with same cast and again directed by James Macdonald; revival of the 1998 production of *Crave*, again directed by Vicky Featherstone. Rehearsed readings also took place of *Phaedra's Love* and *Cleansed*.
2002	February: Sarah Kane Festival, Madrid, Spain. Productions of *Blasted* and *Crave* staged at the Teatro Pradillo.
–	7 March: *Blasted*, Glasgow Citizens Theatre, Scotland; director, Kenny Miller.
–	27 March: Production of *4.48 Psychosis* in Vienna, directed by James Macdonald.
–	1 October: Théâtre des Bouffes du Nord, Paris, *4.48 Psychosis* with the French actress Isabelle Huppert; director, Claude Régie. The production toured to several French cities as well as Portugal during 2003. Huppert reprised the role in September 2005 and the production toured to Brazil, America, Germany and Italy.
–	23 September: Citizens Theatre, Glasgow, Scotland *4.48 Psychosis*; director, Julie Austin.
2003	2 October: *Crave*, Battersea Arts Centre, London; director, Matt Peover. Production revived February and March 2004.
2004	October–November: Touring revival of James

	Macdonald's Royal Court production of *4.48 Psychosis* in America.
2005	May–June: Sarah Kane Season at the Schaubühne Theatre in Berlin, which included a revival of Thomas Ostermeier's 2000 production of *Crave* as well as Ostermeier directing a new production of *Blasted* that had made its debut at the Schaubühne on 16 March. Other productions included Christina Paulhofer's *Phaedra's Love*, Benedict Andrews' *Cleansed* and Falk Richter's *4.48 Psychosis*.
–	20 October: *Phaedra's Love*, Bristol Old Vic; director, Anne Tipton. The production transferred to the Barbican, London, as part of the Young Genius Season 16–26 November.
–	2 November: Oxford Stage Company's production of *Cleansed*, Arcola Theatre, London; director, Sean Holmes.
2006	21 February: *4.48 Psychosis*, Tangram Theatre, Old Red Lion, London; director Daniel Goldman. The production transferred to the Arcola Theatre, 24 April–20 May.
	28 March 2006–3 February 2007: Graeae's *Blasted* UK tour; directors Jenny Sealey and Alex Bulmer.
–	7–11 November: Visit to the Barbican, London, of Thomas Ostermeier's 2005 Berlin production of *Blasted*.

A Chronology of World History, 1989–1999

1989   Communist regimes toppled by revolutions in
        Eastern Europe; fall of the Berlin Wall; pro-
        democracy demonstrations in Tiananmen Square
        savagely repressed by Chinese authorities; major
        earthquakes in San Francisco; fatwa declared on
        Salman Rushdie for his novel *The Satanic Verses*;
        Community Charge (Poll Tax) introduced in
        Scotland; IRA bomb kills ten marines in Deal,
        Kent.

1990   Reunification of Germany; Boris Yeltsin elected
        president of Russian republic; Nelson Mandela
        freed from jail; Iraq invades Kuwait; poll tax
        introduced in UK; Margaret Thatcher resigns as
        prime minister – replaced by John Major; electric-
        ity industry privatised; Iraq 'supergun' seized by
        UK customs.

1991   Mikhail Gorbachev ousted in communist coup –
        subsequently resigns; Soviet Union dissolves and is
        replaced by commonwealth of independent states;
        civil war begins in former Yugoslavia – Serbia
        attacks Croatia and Slovenia to prevent them
        becoming republics; war against Iraq; beating of
        Rodney King by Los Angeles police officers; UK
        property tax replaces poll tax; Britain opts out of
        European single currency.

1992   Series of arms limitation talks (START2);
        European Community recognises independence of
        Croatia and Slovenia; Serbs surround Sarajevo
        and 'ethnic cleansing' of Bosnian Muslims take

place; US troops enter Somalia to secure Mogadishu; single market created in Europe; John Major elected Prime Minister; UK government forced to devalue sterling after 'Black Wednesday'; IRA Omagh bombing kills seven Protestants and Baltic Exchange destroyed in City of London.

1993   David Koresh and followers of the Davidian cult die during FBI raid on their headquarters at Waco Texas; World Wide Web opened up to non-computer specialists; UK ratification of the Maastricht Treaty; IRA bombings in Warrington and City of London – 'Downing Street Declaration' signed; privatisation of British Rail; murder of black teenager Stephen Lawrence.

1994   Nelson Mandela becomes president of South Africa; Yasser Arafat returns to Palestine after twenty-seven years in exile; Russia signs NATO peace accord; rival tribal genocide in Rwanda, Africa; Russia invades the breakaway state of Chechnya; ceasefire agreed in Northern Ireland; John Major's 'Back to Basics' campaign in public life; death of Labour opposition leader John Smith – succeeded by Tony Blair; first women priests ordained in Church of England.

1995   Assassination of Israeli prime minister Yitzhac Rabin; Taliban fighters besiege Afghanistan capital Kabul; Serbian forces attack Zagreb and commit atrocities in the UN-controlled enclave of Srebrenica; NATO bombing of Serbia; Bosnian peace accord signed in Paris; John Major resigns and is re-elected leader of the Conservative Party; Labour opposition leader Tony Blair wins Clause Four debate over party commitment to state ownership; broadcasting ban on the IRA lifted.

1996   Yasser Arafat becomes first president of the Palestinian Authority; Bill Clinton re-elected US president; US troops enter Bosnia as peace-keeping force; Russia signs peace treaty over Chechnya; eighteen tourists killed by Islamic terrorists in Egypt; Taliban capture Kabul; IRA bomb Canary Wharf in London; BSE crisis in UK and EC beef export ban; school shooting massacre in Dunblane, Scotland.

1997   Los Angeles riots in response to acquittal of four police officers for assault of Rodney King – fifty-eight people killed and over 2,000 injured; expulsion of weapons inspectors from Iraq; British leave Hong Kong; Israel begins withdrawal from Hebron; Labour government wins general election with significant majority; Scottish and Welsh devolution approved by referendum; *Sensation* exhibition at the Royal Academy London; death of Diana, Princess of Wales in a car crash; cloning of 'Dolly' the sheep.

1998   US embassies in Nairobi and Dar-es-Salaam bombed – Osama bin Laden suspected; Zimbabwe President Robert Mugabe orders confiscation of white-owned farms; President Clinton impeached; 'Million Man March' in Washington DC to draw attention to racial discrimination in USA; air strikes on Iraq; former Chilean dictator General Pinochet detained in the UK; Good Friday Agreement in Northern Ireland.

1999   President Clinton acquitted in impeachment trial; Euro currency launched in eleven countries; NATO bombs Kosovo followed by peace plan and installation of NATO peace-keeping troops; shootings by two former students at Columbine High School, Colorado; Scottish Parliament and Welsh Assembly open; MacPherson Report talks of 'institutional racism' in UK.

Preface

In November 2006, the Barbican Centre in London staged a
production of Sarah Kane's *Blasted*. Ostensibly, there was
nothing significant about this event. The play had been widely
recognised as one of the key British plays of the 1990s, and so
the decision for the Barbican to revive *Blasted* seemed logical.
Yet it did not hail from a British company, but rather the
Berlin Schaubühne Theatre's 2005 production directed by
Thomas Ostermeier. This, too, may appear unexceptional,
given the Barbican's reputation for hosting international
work, yet at the one-day symposium organised to coincide
with the production, the visiting German contingent expressed
their bemusement concerning Kane's reputation in her home
country. At the time of writing, all five of her plays – *Blasted*
(1995), *Phaedra's Love* (1996), *Cleansed* (1998), *Crave* (1999)
and *4.48 Psychosis* (2000) – are part of the Schaubühne's
repertoire, and Kane is regarded as one of the most significant
European dramatists to have emerged in recent times.
However in Britain no such unanimous accord exists, and
despite the plays being frequently studied and performed in
schools (at sixth-form level), colleges, universities and drama
schools, professional productions are comparatively rare and
confined mainly to London venues rather than major regional
theatres. Whereas the widespread popularity of Kane's work
in Germany has come via regional productions, in Britain
(despite a few notable exceptions) the plays have not become
part of an established repertoire. It is not difficult to understand why: the disturbing subject matter with its depiction of
sex and violence, together with an uncompromising experimentation in dramatic form, are perhaps guaranteed to

alienate regional audiences who, unlike their metropolitan counterparts, are less frequently exposed to such drama.

Yet this volume is part of a series that includes studies on playwrights with international reputations including Samuel Beckett, Caryl Churchill and Harold Pinter. While such inclusion demonstrates the recognition that Kane now merits within the canon of modern drama, it also serves to highlight notable differences in her work from those of her peers. Harold Pinter himself expressed admiration for her work, calling British critics 'way out of their league'[1] in their myopic reactions to *Blasted*. A significant difference is that Kane's reputation, unlike the long careers that Pinter, Beckett and Churchill have sustained, is founded on just five stage plays and a short film written over less than a four-year period. Despite a slim collection of work, a large and growing body of criticism has emerged, and one that shows every sign of challenging the exhaustive scholarship that already exists in Beckett, Churchill and Pinter studies.

Sarah Kane's agent Mel Kenyon believes that with the five plays 'the body of work was absolutely complete'[2] and that she could not have gone any further as a writer. Other commentators such as Michael Billington talk about a sense of incompleteness and lost promise in response to Kane's untimely end; although, here, Billington's flattering assessment seems odd, coming as it does from a person who in his 1995 review of *Blasted* described the play as 'naive tosh' and a 'farrago'.[3]

This contentious relationship to critical opinion and the theatre canon in general has been a feature of Kane's work right from the outset. While the 1995 premiere of *Blasted* at London's Royal Court was lambasted as 'the Nightmare on Sloane Square'[4] by British critics, almost simultaneously her European counterparts (especially those in Germany) were already according the play serious critical attention. It is in this context that the puzzlement of the German visitors at the Barbican becomes understandable. For British audiences, Kane's plays are still associated with gratuitous acts of sex and violence; she is also seen to represent a troubling break within a tradition of female British play writing. Her work is said to have been theatre's chief contribution to the brief cultural period of the mid 1990s known as 'Cool Britannia'. Sarah Kane has also become the tortured artist who immortalised herself through suicide.

The aim of this volume is to dispel some of the shibboleths that have grown up around Sarah Kane the writer and Sarah Kane the person. The volume is divided into three sections: the introduction sets Kane's life and career in a historical context to do with the politics and culture of the decade in which her work was first produced – the 1990s. The introduction also outlines and assesses the current (and often paradoxical) situation regarding Kane's critical reputation both in Britain and internationally. Each of the five plays (and one film) she produced from 1995 to 1999 will also be discussed.

The second part of the volume, 'Kane on Kane', is a digest of interviews and journalism. Some of these have been published elsewhere, but much of the material appears here for the first time, and includes Kane's opinions on a diverse range of subjects; these range from views regarding her own work and aspects of theatre in general to the feminism of Andrea Dworkin and the behaviour of the late Tory minister Alan Clark. The material is arranged thematically and, although I have included a number of endnotes to clarify and provide information about names and subjects discussed, the section is largely free from critical commentary. The aim of this approach is to allow Kane's own voice and opinions to emerge clearly.

The third section consists of new interviews with those involved in Kane's work. These range from critic Aleks Sierz, academic Dan Rebellato and literary agent Mel Kenyon to those who engage with the work directly in the theatre: these include directors Ian Rickson and Jeremy Weller; actors, Diana Kent, Jo McInnes, Suzan Sylvester and Dave Tool; and dramaturges Jens Hilje and Maja Zade. These interviews serve to contextualise Kane's work and reputation in terms of the collaboration that is always necessary in theatre. Here, an emphasis is placed on the particular challenges that the plays present to directors and performers; in this context they can be read comparatively in terms of Kane's thoughts concerning the realisation of her own work and theatre practice in general.

Graham Saunders, Bristol.
January 2009

I

Introduction

Sarah Kane's playwriting career begins with an entrance and closes with an exit. In her debut *Blasted*, the two central protagonists, Ian and Cate, enter through the door of a hotel room '*so expensive it could be anywhere in the world*' (1) and in her final play, *4.48 Psychosis*, a speaker prepares the audience/reader to 'watch me vanish' (244). Just as speculation that one of Prospero's closing speeches ('Our revels now are ended', 4:1,148), from *The Tempest* (1611),[1] is a direct address from Shakespeare announcing his retirement from the stage, the speaker's last lines in *4.48 Psychosis*, 'please open the curtains' (245), make it tempting to see this as Kane's own theatricalised exit or goodbye.

Interpreted as such, it might first appear that Kane's work follows a neat trajectory that can be summarised through the metaphor of a stage direction. Direct engagement with the plays in performance, however, often leads to very different responses: like the unsettling experience of the Leeds hotel room that later undergoes catastrophic change in *Blasted*, audiences have found that experiencing Sarah Kane's theatre takes them into unfamiliar and disturbing territory. Here they encounter situations constructed around extremes of love and cruelty, where bizarre spectacles of suffering are inscribed on tortured and abused bodies. Yet out of such pain, there often emerges a sense of honesty, hope and, at times, even beauty. Kane's last two plays, *Crave* and *4.48 Psychosis*, move away from such overtly physical displays of love and suffering; nor are their entrances and exits based on traditional stage directions, but are more like metaphorical openings that allow the spectator/reader glimpses into fractured mindscapes rather than the familiarity of the everyday.

One notable feature of Kane's early work was the anger and mystification it aroused from critics and audiences alike. The British reviews of *Blasted* in particular were notorious for their hostility. Jack Tinker's melodramatic byline ('This Disgusting Feast of Filth', *Daily Mail*, 19 January 1995) has subsequently entered into theatre-lore, and UK critics generally failed to appreciate or understand her work until relatively late with *Crave* in 1998.

This lapse of several years before finally achieving critical recognition is nothing new; dramatists including Harold Pinter and Edward Bond have both had to wait for opinion to catch up with their work. As has been noted, while Sarah Kane's work is performed constantly worldwide, an anomalous situation exists in Britain. Despite recent revivals such as Anne Tipton's production of *Phaedra's Love* (Bristol Old Vic/Barbican Pit), Sean Holmes's *Cleansed* (Arcola Theatre, London) in 2005, and Graeae's touring production of *Blasted* in 2006–7, professional stagings since her death have been rare.

Notwithstanding the relative scarcity of productions at home, Kane's status as a dramatist in Europe and beyond continues to grow. Yet, this process of canonisation following her death in 1999 contains its own inherent dangers: as one reviewer of the 2002 Glasgow Citizen's production of *Blasted* observed, the play has now virtually become, 'a sacred cow you attack at your peril'.[2] The theatre director Dominic Dromgoole and critic Aleks Sierz have also addressed the short sightedness of this lionisation. They have pointed out that Kane's work is not immune from criticism and that the plays can be subject to self-indulgence and adolescent petulance, together with a lack of formal characterisation and a narrow obsessiveness in its range of subject matter.[3] Yet, accusations of self-indulgence can often be mistaken for a writer's uncompromising personal vision that in retrospect enables new ways of perceiving the world.

It is also worth considering that one of Kane's main intentions from *Blasted* onwards was to break down traditional forms of characterisation based on the conventions of realism and naturalism. However, the charge that Kane's drama occasionally displays an immaturity does carry more validity: despite generally enthusiastic responses to the 2001 Sarah Kane season at the Royal Court, *Blasted* was described as 'the worst kind of student drama' by one panellist on the BBC2 television programme *Newsnight Review*.[4] Reactionary, perhaps, yet lines such as 'Fuck God. Fuck the monarchy' (95), from *Phaedra's Love*, and 'Fuck you for rejecting me by never being there' (215), from *4.48 Psychosis*, display signs of an adolescent sensibility – one which strikes an immediate chord with Kane's wide student following. Yet, it should also be remembered that Kane was only twenty-three when she wrote *Blasted* and, in the main, her work is remarkable for its depth, maturity and control.

Kane's popularity abroad has also not escaped criticism. In one of a series of newspaper articles looking at the state of European theatre in 2003, John Mahoney singled out the work of the Royal Court, and Sarah Kane in particular, as having a detrimental effect on indigenous theatre: according to Mahoney, frequent revivals ossify into a formulaic pattern leading to 'a dull repetitive and characterless "brand" of theatre, whose imposing shadow stretches right across the continent'.[5] Such accusations hold little credence when one considers Kane's involvement in the Royal Court's International Summer School during 1997–8. Elyse Dodgson, who has run the scheme since 1989, noted that participants involved in the 1998 workshop run by Kane subsequently went on to become leading practitioners in their own countries.[6] Moreover, the success of Kane's work throughout Europe saw a return to new theatre writing and away from the tradition of director-led reinterpretations of classical work. Subsequently, a new generation of theatre writers emerged including Marius von Mayenburg and Juan Mayorga. Kane's friend (and director of her 1996 film *Skin*) Vincent O'Connell defended her success in Europe by responding in a letter to the *Guardian*, arguing that, rather than representing a sinister form of theatrical glob-alisation, the frequency of productions confirmed their cross-cultural relevance.[7]

Another persistent accusation has been that the repetition of themes in Kane's work such as the connections between love and violence risks the plays becoming self-referential to the point of cliché. The Irish writer Chris Lee's short parody of Kane's work entitled *Crushed* illustrated this characteristic in a style that, I would argue, only served to confirm the voice of an original and recognisable artist:

A **head** *appears.*
Head: Fuck. Cunt. Fuck. Cunting fucking cunting cunting fuck.
A man walks on with a baseball bat. He bends down and kisses the head. He stands up. He smashes the head with the baseball bat. He puts down the bat. He pulls down his pants and urinates on the head. He waits. He defecates on the head. He waits. He masturbates and ejaculates on the head. A tree immediately appears where the head had been.
Tree: At last I have truly known love.
Suddenly the tree explodes. The man explodes. The theatre explodes. The world explodes.
Fuck you all.

Just as the work can become appropriated by parody, so too can the writer – especially if she is no longer alive. Peter Morris made this point explicitly in an article entitled 'The Brand of Kane', written a year after her death in 1999. While recognising her talent, Morris observed that a process was already underway whereby both the work and the playwright had become 'recon-figured as a kind of easily assimilated icon, like Duchamp's uri-nal now placidly enshrined in some vast museum'.[8]

It is also tempting to see the dramatist Martin Crimp's short essay written in 2004, entitled 'When the Writer Kills Himself', as a piece about the idolatry surrounding Sarah Kane after her suicide. The essay concerns the predicament of living dramatists struggling for recognition against the reputation of a recently dead anonymous writer who 'is filling theatres and making the universities hum'.⁹ Crimp's essay warned of the dangers that come from lionising a writer. Undoubtedly, Kane's work and reputation have tended to dominate the story of playwriting in the 1990s. For some, she has become *the* dramatist of that decade, thereby marginalising other important writers. Crimp's essay also suggested that a writer's reputation will suffer when the manner of their death becomes the yardstick by which their work is judged.

At the same time, Kane's association with the culture of the 1990s has never been an easy or convincing one, despite claims made for her inclusion within the short-lived period of 'Cool Britannia'. Here, young artists in art, theatre, film and music were grouped together under this collective banner and likened to a cultural movement by critics such as Robert Hewison and Ken Urban. In theatre, Kane was one of the first to be placed with other young dramatists such as Jez Butterworth, Mark Ravenhill and Judy Upton who shared a preoccupation with staging acts of extreme violence and sexuality. These writers were the subject of Aleks Sierz's influential book *In-Yer-Face Theatre: British Drama Today*, which coined the term 'in-yer-face', to describe the subject matter and dramatic form used by many of these new playwrights.¹⁰ Undoubtedly, Kane's work is preoccupied with such depictions of sex and violence, yet it differs significantly from Jez Butterworth's *Mojo* that premiered the same year as *Blasted*. Whereas the gruesome acts of staged violence in *Mojo* set out to deliberately amuse and entertain its audiences, in *Blasted* violence was used to carefully build up a number of connections between the causes of domestic sexual violence eventually culminating in the violence of warfare. Hence, *Blasted* becomes a far more ambitious play than many of its contemporaries – moving from narrow definitions of British nationalism through the character of Ian to later events that dramatise the effects of war atrocities on the human psyche and issues of personal and spiritual redemption.

Kane's plays also differ in their relationship to 'Cool Britannia' itself. While contemporary references are scattered throughout Kane's work (football in *Blasted*, the Beatles/the Smiths lyrics in *Cleansed* and *4.48 Psychosis*), her plays always followed a dogmatic personal vision that had little to do with the explicit concerns of 1990s Britain. Whereas the *'distant sound of coins clattering'*[11] from a fruit machine arcade in Mark Ravenhill's *Shopping and Fucking* (1996) becomes one of the key dramatic motifs articulating consumerist culture in late 1990s Britain, the blinded Ian occupying an infant's grave in *Blasted* is more reminiscent of imagery drawn from renaissance drama or the work of Samuel Beckett. In general, her work also eschews the numerous film and television references used by contemporaries such as Jez Butterworth and Martin McDonagh. Rather, many of the cultural allusions in Kane's work make use of older literary sources such as the King James Bible and T. S. Eliot's poem *The Wasteland* (1922). Both her themes and subject matter are far removed from the girl gangs we find inhabiting the work of Judy Upton (*Ashes and Sand*) and Rebecca Prichard (*Essex Girls* and *Yard Gal*), or the disaffected urbanites who haunt the plays of Patrick Marber (*Dealer's Choice* and *Closer*) and Nick Grosso (*Sweetheart* and *Peaches*).

If Ravenhill's characters question whether human subjectivity is real or induced through drugs and consumerist culture, Kane's characters often have a romantic sensibility predicated on emotional excess. Even desensitised figures such as Ian and Hippolytus are *made* (often violently) painfully to experience the world in order to understand themselves. While Kane and Ravenhill do converge via an exploration of themes of sexual abuse, the search for love and a shared concern with characters who self-mutilate, Kane's drama concentrates on existential questions such as the loss of religious faith, the nature and causes of violence and the effects of a nihilistic sensibility.

The difficulty in attempting to assess Kane's reputation is further complicated by the claims made not just for her importance within a specific 'school' of playwriting in the 1990s but also within a wider tradition of post-war British drama. For instance, Ken Urban argued that her plays 'altered the landscape of British theatre in the 1990s',[12] and Aleks Sierz went even further when he said that *Blasted* 'led to a revolution in sensibility like the one initiated in 1956 with [John Osborne's] *Look Back in Anger*'.[13] In retrospect, such claims are exaggerated. *Blasted* never made the same inroads into public consciousness, nor did it refashion the style and content of British cinema and television in the same way as *Look Back in Anger*: Kane's work did not alter the prevailing dramatic form of social realism that still dominates British playwriting today. Likewise, declarations that there existed an alternative school of angry young women in the 1990s (including Kane, Prichard and Upton) have also been dismissed as 'spurious and flashy' by John McRae and Ronald Carter.[14] Elaine Aston in her study of female English dramatists in the 1990s noted how quickly Kane's work became appropriated within the pantheon of the Royal Court 'angry young men'.[15] This is certainly true, but it is worth adding that this adoption of an overtly 'male' sensibility was something that Kane seemed actively to promote, deliberately appearing to remove herself from any association or tradition of women dramatists to have emerged since 1956.

This appropriation of a masculine tradition and refusal to be associated with a female playwriting culture has been questioned by David Ian Rabey, who drew attention to similarities between *Blasted* and Sarah Daniels' influential play *Masterpieces* (1983)[16] – and it is worth pointing out that Kane's work is sometimes far closer to a recognisable feminist playwriting tradition than would initially suggest itself. For instance, striking affinities can be found between *Blasted* and another earlier work associated with feminist concerns – Claire McIntyre's *My Heart's a Suitcase* (1990). Here, the television news story of rape and murder ('The body of the missing Petworth newspaper girl Tracy Hogg has been discovered in a shallow grave in woodland just five hundred yards from her home')[17] bears close similarities with Ian's journalistic account of the murder of Samantha Scrace (12–13). Further echoes exist between the inexplicable appearance of the Soldier in *Blasted* and the figure of Baggage in McIntyre's play.[18] Such connections, together with a preoccupation with male sexual violence perpetuated against women through rape, locate Kane far closer to a previous generation of women dramatists. This also goes some way to challenging Kane's own often quoted refusal to either categorise herself as a woman dramatist, or recognise that her plays explored issues directly related to sexual politics.[19]

What this brief assessment sets out to demonstrate are the problems that exist in reaching a consensus or understanding of Sarah Kane's work. This situation has become further obscured by the circumstances of Kane's death, which quickly brought with it inevitable associations of the young tragic female artist. Mary Luckhurst drew a parallel with the suicide of poet Sylvia Plath, and observed that afterwards her work became critically disseminated almost exclusively through the narrow focus of gender and mental health.[20] While this reading will inevitably be attached to the work (especially the later plays), the section in this volume entitled 'Kane on Kane' is a corrective to such an approach. By collecting together interviews and her own journalism, it presents a space for the playwright to speak for herself.

Life

Sarah Kane was born on 3 February 1971 in Brentwood, Essex, and spent her childhood in the nearby village of Kelvedon Hatch. Her parents were both journalists, although her mother gave up full-time work to look after both Sarah and her older brother, Simon.

Kane became interested in theatre at an early age and acted with the Basildon Youth Theatre group. After attending a local school (Shenfield Comprehensive), in 1989 Kane went to Bristol University where she studied drama. It was during this period that she first began writing. In August 1991, Kane wrote and performed in a short piece entitled *Comic Monologue* at the Edinburgh Festival. This was part of a series of written/devised work called *Dreams/Screams and Silences*, performed by a group of Bristol University students who had formed under the name Sore Throats Theatre Company. July 1992 saw Kane graduating from university with a first-class honours degree. During this time, she began to develop an embryonic version of *Blasted* and revisited the Edinburgh Festival in a new show with Sore Throats Theatre Company. By now, the company consisted of just Kane and her friend Vincent O'Connell. The show was called *Dreams/Screams 2*. Alongside short plays by O'Connell, Kane wrote and performed two new monologues entitled *Starved* and *What She Said*. At the Edinburgh Festival that year, Kane attended Jeremy Weller's Grassmarket Project's *Mad*, a devised play performed by people who had suffered from mental illness. This performance subsequently had a profound effect on Kane's ideas about theatre.

In October 1992, she enrolled on an MA in playwriting at Birmingham University. The course, which had been set up in 1989 by the dramatist David Edgar, was generally not a happy experience for Kane. Yet, by March 1993, a first draft of *Blasted* had been written. It was performed in extract at the university's Allardyce Nicoll Studio Theatre on 3 July 1993, with student actors and a professional director, Pete Wynne-Wilson, and was played up until the point Cate performs fellatio on Ian (30). Like the Royal Court production in 1995, *Blasted* divided the audience, but it impressed the literary agent Mel Kenyon, who attended the performance, and *Blasted* was taken up as an option by the Royal Court, with a rehearsed reading taking place on 29 January 1994.

Kane took up the post of literary associate at the Bush Theatre, London, in March. By August she had unexpectedly quit the job. Dominic Dromgoole, its artistic director at the time, humorously recalled, 'It was only a couple of days later that we realised she'd walked out. She'd left an indignant note, but unfortunately none of us ever found it.'[21] During the autumn of that year, Kane wrote several drafts of the film script, *Skin*.

The year 1995 began with the premiere of *Blasted* at the Royal Court Theatre Upstairs. The play previewed from 12 January; the infamous press night that launched the barrage of media attention was on 18 January. Kane kept a low profile during this febrile time, although she did give an interview to the journalist/playwright Clare Bayley for the *Independent*.[22]

In May of that year Kane participated in an exchange programme set up by the Royal Court with New Dramatists in New York, and during that summer final drafts of *Skin* were completed. Filming took place during September and it was screened at the London Film Festival the following month. The latter part of 1995 was devoted to starting work on *Phaedra's Love*, which arose out of a commission from the Gate Theatre in Notting Hill, London. Kane ended up replacing the assigned director, Cath Mattock, and the play was first performed on 15 May 1996. That August Kane became writer-in-residence at London-based Paines Plough, a company specialising in new writing. The residency lasted until March 1998, and it was here that *Crave* was produced in August 1998.

In February 1997, Kane participated in the Royal Court's annual International Exchange Programme with a production of *Phaedra's Love* at the Deutsche Theater Baracke in Berlin. The following month a reading of *Crave* was performed at Paines Plough, although it was given under the pseudonym of 'Marie Kelvedon' – a name constructed from Kane's middle name and childhood village. That year also marked Kane's first voluntary admission to the Royal Maudsley Hospital in London for severe depression, although by October she was well enough to direct a production of Georg Büchner's *Woyzeck* at the Gate Theatre.

The year 1998 was a productive one, with two new plays. *Cleansed* was the first of her plays to be produced on the main stage of the Royal Court, although due to refurbishment it was actually staged at the Court's temporary home, the Duke of York's Theatre. The remainder of that year involved Kane leading writing workshops for other dramatists: these included a British Council-sponsored event in Amsterdam during May, while the following month brought Kane to the Varna Festival in Bulgaria where she assisted the Royal Court's International Play Development Programme by setting up a writers' group in the capital, Sofia. July and August were devoted to leading playwriting workshops at the Royal Court's International Residency in London with dramatists from seventeen different countries.

In August *Crave* premiered. Kane's second new play that year was performed at the Traverse Theatre as part of the Edinburgh Festival, before transferring to the Royal Court Theatre Upstairs (temporarily located at the Ambassadors Theatre) during September. The production toured to Ireland and Europe. For five performances, in Maastricht and Copenhagen, Kane took on the role of C. In November, Kane worked with Andalusian writers in Seville, Spain, again as part of the Royal Court International Play Development Programme. That same month she won an Arts Foundation Fellowship for Playwriting.

While 1998 became a creative watershed, and one where British critical opinion about her work started to change, the beginning of 1999 was marked by another serious bout of depression. After an unsuccessful suicide attempt, Kane was admitted to King's College Hospital in London, but between two and three o'clock on the morning of 20 February she hanged herself. Her final play, *4.48 Psychosis*, was performed posthumously at the Royal Court Theatre Upstairs on 23 June 2000.

1989–1999: Political, Historical and Cultural Context

> If the word in the eighties was 'me', and in the nineties 'it',
> in the millennium it's 'ish'. Everything has to be vague and
> qualified. Substance used to be important, then style was
> everything. Now it's all just faking it (Irvine Welsh, *Porno*,
> p. 374).

Sarah Kane and the so-called 'in-yer-face' generation of British
dramatists that emerged in the mid 1990s were shaped by two
opposing forces: political revolution globally and political iner-
tia at home. The former came with the sudden and unexpected
collapse of the Berlin Wall that divided (communist) East and
(democratic) West Berlin in 1989. The reunification of East and
West Germany took place the following year. The physical dis-
mantling of the Berlin Wall led to a rapid collapse of other
communist Eastern European regimes in Bulgaria, Czechoslo-
vakia, Hungary, Poland and Romania.

In 1991, the Russian Soviet Union (USSR) also dissolved. Its
last communist president, Mikhail Gorbachev, resigned and in
elections that year was replaced by Boris Yeltsin.

One other bloody consequence of the overthrow of commu-
nism during 1991 arose in the former Yugoslavia. Civil war
broke out after Serbia fought neighbouring Croatia and
Slovenia both to prevent their independence and also as a
reaction to perceived threats to Serbian strongholds in the
Krajina region of Croatia. After the European Community
recognised the sovereignty of both countries, during June and
July of 1991, Serbian forces surrounded and then captured the
Croatian capital Dubrovnik.

A new phase in the conflict took place in April 1992 when
neighbouring Bosnia also declared independence, and a
renewed war broke out between Serbia, Croatia and Bosnia.
Sarajevo, the capital of Bosnia Herzegovina, was besieged.
Despite troops being deployed by the United Nations and its
official designation as a safe area, Serbian forces carried out
what was euphemistically called 'ethnic cleansing' of Bosnian

Muslims in enclaves such as Srebrenica, with the mass killing of an estimated seven thousand Muslim men. The siege of Srebrenica was a major catalyst to the writing of *Blasted*.[23] While informed by actual events, such as those recounted by the Soldier outlining the evacuation of civilians ('Saw thousands of people packing into trucks like pigs,' 50) and atrocities committed during the conflict ('Went to a house just outside town,' 43), the play is not a direct engagement or commentary on the war itself.

As Berlin was united in 1990, the same year saw the fall of the British prime minister Margaret Thatcher. For Kane, born in 1971, the Thatcher administration had been in power for much of her childhood and early adulthood since its election in 1979. Mrs Thatcher's deposition by her own ministers had come about mainly through her unbending advocacy for the replacement of local rates for council services by the Community Charge, more commonly known as the Poll Tax.

Despite Mrs Thatcher's fall from power, the political landscape in Britain remained largely unchanged. John Major was elected by his party to replace her, and against expectations won a fourth conservative victory in 1992, albeit with a narrow parliamentary majority. Yet, shortly after its election the Major government was wracked by internal dissent, much of it emanating from the so-called 'Eurosceptic' wing of his party. Added to this was a succession of scandals (both sexual and financial), amongst various ministers and MPs, which undermined John Major's leadership to such an extent that, in June 1995, he resigned and put himself up for re-election as prime minister in a bid to resolve the matter. Although he gained a majority, internal divisions still bedevilled his administration and it was of little surprise to many that on 1 May 1997 the Labour Party under its leader Tony Blair won the general election with a significant majority of elected MPs.

Girl Power, In-Yer-Face and Unmade Beds: British Culture in the 1990s

The stasis in British politics throughout the 1990s was reflected in its culture. The two strands memorably came together when such organs of the Establishment as *The Spectator* magazine and BBC Radio 4's current affairs programme *Today* interviewed pop group The Spice Girls, ostensibly for their political views. Some saw this as simply another feature of post-modernism, with distinctions breaking down between 'high' and 'popular' culture. The playwright David Edgar summed up the situation in the following way:

> It is an exaggeration to say that the counter-culture [of the 1960s and early 1970s] set out to replace *Hamlet*, Keats and Beethoven with Dario Fo, Bob Dylan and Velvet Underground but ended up giving a progressive imprimatur to *Casualty*, Jeffrey Archer and The Spice Girls. But it's not *too* far from the truth.[24]

By the mid 1990s, the phrase 'style over substance' was used to describe both British politics and culture. This reached its zenith during the period known as 'Cool Britannia', which assumed a brief prominence following the early months of Tony Blair's election victory in May 1997.

No longer the party of opposition, Labour were quick to associate themselves with the renaissance in youthful creativity taking place in the arts, which centred on pop music and art. These included beat groups such as Blur, Oasis and Suede and the so-called Young British Artists (YBAs) such as Damien Hirst, Marcus Harvey and Chris Ofili.

While certain parallels were drawn between Sarah Kane, the in-yer-face dramatists and the YBAs – mainly through the tactics each employed to deliberately provoke their respective audiences – the new voices in theatre differed markedly from their contemporaries in the art world through their modes of representation and the reactions they wished to incite. These intrinsic differences served to disassociate most new theatre

14

writing from inclusion within the umbrella term 'Cool Britannia'. For instance, whereas Kane drew inspiration from the war in Bosnia for *Blasted*, or the death camps of Auschwitz for *Cleansed*, the YBAs looked to advertising techniques, such as those used in the 1991 Benetton campaign, where the clothing brand was marketed through a series of highly charged images such as a man dying of AIDS, and a nun kissing a priest.[25]

The new plays being produced during 'Cool Britannia' were often in direct opposition to the celebratory mood of the times. Dramatists such as David Eldridge and Che Walker presented a far bleaker picture of Britain than New Labour's confident vision. A clear example of this emerged in 1998 when Mark Ravenhill's *Shopping and Fucking* – frequently cited as theatre's main contribution to 'Cool Britannia' – was publicly condemned by Education Secretary David Blunkett after going on a British Council-funded European tour. Despite admitting that he had not seen the play, Blunkett castigated the tour as a waste of taxpayers' money. The characters in *Shopping and Fucking*, with their dependence on drugs, shallow consumerism and 'lick and go' sex, become an unwelcome narrative against the prevailing representation of a reborn and energetic Britain that New Labour were so keen to promote abroad.

Media commentators, writing at the end of the 1980s, made predictions that the 1990s would become 'the caring decade', after Thatcherism. Ultimately, such sentiments proved fallacious. All too often, 'caring' in the 1990s seemed to constitute a blend of mawkish sentimentality (displayed at its peak immediately after the death of Princess Diana in August 1997) or flaky New Age ethics.

The so-called 'caring decade' also failed to be represented in its culture, where all too often it seemed preoccupied with images of humiliation, cruelty and violence. This ranged from the prurient voyeurism of reality television shows, such as *Big Brother*, to Damien Hirst's artworks involving preserved animals – a shark in *The Physical Impossibility of Death in the*

Mind of Someone Living (1991) and a sheep in *Mother and Child Divided* (1993). Beneath the brash and glittering mantle of 'Cool Britannia' lurked images of the cruel and aberrant, often cynically portrayed in a clinical and distanced manner that glamorised their disturbing subject matter. In contrast, plays such *Blasted* and *Shopping and Fucking* used their imagery in order to explore societal tensions and injustices; here the outlandish and violent were based on a methodology of cause and effect, rather than the effect itself a substitution for the rationale.

Theatre's relative distance from the 'Cool Britannia' project was, in retrospect, beneficial. Neither Kane nor her fellow dramatists ever dominated the media as a recognisable group in the same way as Britart or Britpop. This relative anonymity allowed Kane's work in particular to develop independently of any particular cultural moment or event. While undoubtedly certain works from Britpop and Britart will transcend the period in which they were created, the aesthetics of style over substance all too easily resembles the 'tawdry shell'[26] of the Millennium Dome – a grand project associated with New Labour at the end of the 1990s – where the dome was finally host to a disparate and disappointing array of 'attractions'.

Kane's Career in Context

'Shocking Scenes in Sloane Square': *Blasted*

An often-used adjective when it came to assessing the cultural impact of John Osborne's *Look Back in Anger* in 1956 was 'explosive'. In *Blasted*, with its choice of title and stage direction ('*The hotel has been blasted by a mortar bomb*,' 39), this was almost literal and resulted in Kane's debut attaining both immediate notoriety and subsequent recognition as a landmark work.

Blasted is a one-act play of five scenes. It begins with the exploration of an abusive relationship between Ian, a middle-aged journalist who has brought Cate, a much younger former girlfriend to a Leeds hotel room. Ian has organised the meeting for the purposes of seduction, yet despite Cate's protestations their night together culminates in Ian subjecting her to a sexual assault. After Cate escapes through the bathroom window, *Blasted* changes radically in style with the entrance of a nameless Soldier. The room is hit by a mortar bomb and, as both men recover, the Soldier tells Ian of the atrocities he has committed in a civil war that has broken out. We are now no longer sure whether the location is Leeds or elsewhere in the world. The encounter between the pair culminates in the Soldier raping and blinding Ian after which he shoots himself. Cate later returns with a baby that has been entrusted to her care. Although the infant dies Cate buries it and prays for its safe-keeping in the afterlife. Ian is left alone again and time itself breaks down. While whole seasons pass, Ian carries out an increasingly bizarre series of acts that culminates in him eating the buried baby and occupying its makeshift grave. The play ends with Cate returning and feeding Ian with bread, sausage and gin. Ian's final utterance is 'Thank you' (61).

Blasted came at the tail end of a season of plays at the Theatre Upstairs by new young writers at the Royal Court. The 1994 season was noted at the time by several commentators as a promising sign of resurgence in theatre writing, and many of the dramatists subsequently built upon this propitious start. The season included Joe Penhall's *Some Voices*, Michael Wynne's *The Knocky*, Rebecca Prichard's *Essex Girls*, Nick Grosso's *Peaches* and Judy Upton's *Ashes and Sand*. *Blasted* was the last play in the season and limited to a three-week run. Just over a thousand people saw the first production. Ian Rickson, artistic director at the time, observed that fewer people saw *Blasted* in its entire first run than at one performance of Conor McPherson's West End hit *The Weir*.[27]

Blasted was initially associated with a spate of so-called 'lads' plays that same year. These included William Gaminara's *According to Hoyle*, David Greer's *Burning Blue* and Louis

Mellis and David Scinto's *Gangster No.1*. In *Blasted*, Ian is literally representative of a diseased male identity – a crude racist, misogynist and homophobe who is compulsively drinking and smoking himself to death.

Here, verbal abuse leads to Ian's sexual assault upon an unconscious Cate with a gun to her head. Yet underlying Ian's cruelty is a vulnerability, which is revealed after he is raped by the Soldier and becomes reliant on Cate's help. This loss of power is made all the more poignant when one considers how defensively Ian guards his own constructed sense of masculinity earlier in the play. For instance, when Cate asks whether he has ever slept with another man Ian explodes, 'You think I'm a cocksucker? You've seen me. (*He vaguely indicates his groin*). How can you think that?' (19). Later, when he is about to be anally raped, his attacker sardonically observes that Ian is still pathetically attempting to cling to his heterosexual identity:

Soldier Going to fuck you.
Ian No.
Soldier Kill you then.
Ian Fine.
Soldier See. Rather be shot than fucked and shot. (49)

Despite the first half's domestic themes, *Blasted* develops into both a State-of-the-Nation and State-of-Europe play. In an early letter of support in the British press, the Reverend Bob Vernon said that the images in *Blasted* reminded him of the housing estates in his North Shields parish which resembled 'war zones . . . burnt out houses, glass and rubbish littered streets, dazed, tranquillised people trying to survive'.[28] *Blasted* was unique in its willingness to confront and dramatise aspects of the conflict in Yugoslavia and the atrocities associated with that particular war. It also suggested, primarily through the character of Ian and his occupation as a tabloid journalist, our culpability as a nation in allowing the war to continue.

As mentioned, Kane's work has been described as a marketable 'brand', yet *Blasted* never emulated Mark Ravenhill's

Shopping and Fucking the following year, which took up a successful residency in the West End. Ravenhill himself believed
that *Blasted* in some respects 'softened up the critics',[29] and prepared audiences for his own play. Certainly, *Shopping and
Fucking* received a (generally) appreciative critical reception,
whereas *Blasted* drew an unparalleled stream of vitriol from
newspaper critics: as 'a piece of drama it is utterly without dramatic merit',[30] stated one, while another described it as 'a lazy,
tawdry piece of work without an idea in its head beyond an
adolescent desire to shock'.[31] The facile content of many of
these reviews echoed Ian's own style of hack journalism. Phil
Gibby writing in the *Stage* argued that, while *Blasted* was neither well nor badly written, the genuine surprise came from the
hysterical reactions of his fellow critics.[32]

Here, *Blasted* was in good company. Landmark plays, radically new in form or content, have often been met with derision
and protest. Reaction has ranged from the outrage that greeted
the first performance in the UK of Henrik Ibsen's *Ghosts*
(1881) to rioting during a performance of John Millington
Synge's *The Playboy of the Western World* (1907) and the
bored incomprehension that greeted John Arden's *Serjeant
Musgrave's Dance* (1959). With *Blasted*, audiences reacted
with an alarm and ridicule symptomatic of a failure to discern
that the violence they were witnessing had a logical structure.
Aleks Sierz's impression of audience reactions at those early
Royal Court performances are indicative:

> Two people walked out, others hid their eyes, and some gig-
> gled. However, the responses were mixed: some people
> were irritated by what they saw as puerile exhibitionism;
> others were moved by the starkness of the horror or by the
> psychological accuracy of the relationships.[33]

Alongside lurid descriptions of its content, objections were
raised over the play's lack of realism, its elusive and allusive references to the conflict in Bosnia and its structural weaknesses.
Patronising comments were directed at Kane's age and gender.

These reactions were compounded by the play moving suddenly from domestic social realism in the first half to a form of neo-expressionism in the second. By ignoring the careful connections that Kane had made between the two sections, audiences experienced the play as a succession of jolting images that seemed to have no context.

By the time of its 2001 revival, originally hostile critics such as Charles Spencer recognised that 'the atrocities now seem more organic to the play, rather than mere theatrical shock-tactics'.[34]

In retrospect, part of the reason behind *Blasted*'s adverse reception came from Kane's desire to thwart expectations. In the opening scene, the props, '*a large double bed. A mini-bar and champagne on ice. A telephone. A large bouquet of flow-er*s,' and the stage direction, '*A very expensive hotel room in Leeds*' (3), give the impression that *Blasted* belongs to a genre of romantic comedy reminiscent of Noel Coward's *Private Lives* (1933) or Neil Simon's *California Suite* (1978). Such expectations are undercut with Ian's first words as he enters the hotel room, 'I've shat in better places than this' (3). Moreover, each of the props which anticipate romantic love eventually becomes a signifier for self-destruction and violence: the mini-bar becomes a repository for Ian's chronic alcoholism; the bed becomes the location of Cate's sexual assault by Ian; and the bouquet later shown '*ripped apart and scattered around the room*' (24) are symbolic representations of the assault itself.

We are constantly misled by the fact that Ian's insults to Cate are often mixed with protestations of love. This wrong footing extends to its overall structure. Just as we become accustomed to *Blasted* being a realistic play staged in a domestic setting concerning an abusive relationship, the entry of the Soldier and the subsequent bomb blast strips away any vestiges of realism.

These opening moments of *Blasted* show how easy it is to misinterpret the complex meanings inherent in Kane's work. In the original Royal Court production, budgetary restraints and the small playing space meant that it was difficult to replicate the luxury of the hotel interior. Ian's opening lines are possibly meant as a joke, and work on the incongruity of the statement 'I've shat in better places than this' (3) to the plush surroundings of the room. Because the stage set failed to approximate these conditions, Kane's agent observed that 'right from the outset audiences and critics would be likely to misinterpret the play'.[35]

Despite the vehement and almost unanimous critical opprobrium that greeted the play, *Blasted* proved that a work performed in a small studio theatre could create shockwaves that reached way beyond its immediate audience, generating, even, a national news story about the depiction of violence on stage. *Blasted* provides a rare example of how the aberrant, through mass media notoriety, can suddenly find itself occupying, albeit for a short while, a prominent place in mainstream culture.

'No One Burns Me': *Phaedra's Love*

For Kane's second play, the subject matter was drawn from Greek myth. Twentieth-century drama contains a number of significant works either directly or obliquely influenced by elements of the Phaedra story[36] and *Phaedra's Love* is loosely based on the version by Roman playwright, poet and philosopher Seneca. While this one-act drama retains elements from Seneca's version such as Hippolytus' reclusiveness, Kane's play offers a radically different interpretation of the familiar narrative concerning the doomed sexual obsession by the eponymous queen for her stepson Hippolytus.

Kane's retelling of the tragedy imagines a modern British royal family and departs from Seneca's version in reversing the prince's strict chastity. Instead, Hippolytus is involved in a succession of joyless sexual encounters that serves to accentuate his underlying depressive state. In another departure from Seneca, Phaedra is shown to consummate the sexual obsession towards her stepson through performing fellatio. However, Hippolytus brutally rejects her romantic aspirations by telling his stepmother that her daughter, Strophe, has been a past sexual conquest. Phaedra commits suicide, leaving a note accusing

Hippolytus of rape. This act unleashes a series of tragic events that eventually destroys the royal family.

A mob of rioting subjects gathers outside the palace, yet paradoxically this threat of destruction enervates Hippolytus. While in prison, he refuses the Priest's offer of forgiveness and asserts a philosophy of living by a creed of absolute honesty. The play ends with Hippolytus being castrated and disembowelled by his former subjects. As '*A vulture descends and begins to eat his body*,' Hippolytus' last words are 'If there could have been more moments like this' (103).

Phaedra's Love opened sixteen months after *Blasted* in May 1996. It started out as a commission from London's Gate Theatre for Kane to adapt a well-known classical play of her choosing. It is a short play – just over seventy minutes in performance – and consists of eight brief scenes. *Phaedra's Love* is also notable for Kane directing the first production herself.

Phaedra's Love is a very different play from *Blasted*, yet both share several related themes. The abusive and masochistic relationship played out between Ian and Cate is repeated in the interplay between Hippolytus and Phaedra. Ian and Hippolytus are also both nihilistic representations of a masculinity that sees little point to daily existence. Hippolytus complains that 'Life's too long' (79), while Ian's worldview can be summed up by his bitter rejoinder, 'No God. No Father Christmas. No fairies. No Narnia. No fucking nothing' (55). This self-hatred is manifested through the two men being stricken with symbolic pathologies such as the loss of Ian's lung to cancer, which he describes as 'this lump of rotting pork' (11), and Hippolytus' oral gonorrhoea that he deliberately passes on to Phaedra via fellatio (85).

Exactly what constitutes *Phaedra's Love* continues to resonate after her death. For Hippolytus, culpability for his stepmother's suicide signals the death of love. The Priest, who comes to Hippolytus in the hope of hearing him confess and save himself by denying the accusation of rape, believes, 'Love never dies. It evolves . . . Into respect. Consideration' (93). This refers to

Hippolytus' position as a royal prince and guardian of the nation's morality: above all Hippolytus is urged to preserve and continue the dynasty. For Hippolytus these considerations are a betrayal of love and he denounces the Priest as 'dangerous' (93).

Love has brought Hippolytus personal redemption and a grim satisfaction in being the architect responsible for bringing down the corrupt edifice that his family represents. Rather than embracing a Christian God, Hippolytus' sense of personal salvation is gained from Phaedra's death, together with a determination to live and die by a creed of absolute honesty. The Priest observes, 'There is a kind of purity in you' (97), but the Priest by contrast retains a moral pragmatism that wishes to sustain order and power in the earthly life through the system of church and monarchy. He is content to serve two masters simultaneously – God and Hippolytus. This ambiguous morality and shifting loyalty are reflected in the passive act of fellatio the Priest performs on Hippolytus, and which convinces the prince to gladly accept the tragic fate that awaits him.

Phaedra's Love also draws obliquely on contemporary references to the British royal family through parallels between Phaedra and Princess Diana. Just as Hippolytus believes Phaedra sacrificed herself on his behalf (91), a mythology established itself after Diana's death as one who 'had died with her life and her suffering, for the desires of others'.[37]

This exploration of wider public attitudes towards the British monarchy is also found in Hippolytus' abject suspicion towards his subjects. Whereas Phaedra displays snobbery in finding the poverty of her subjects 'charming' (75) through their choice of gifts, Hippolytus sees his birthday celebrations as a sham designed to fool the populace, 'News. Another rape. Child murdered. War somewhere. Few thousand jobs gone. But none of this matters 'cause it's a royal birthday' (74).

The crass sentimentality of the nation's relationship to the royals is mixed with a dangerous volatility. Strophe warns her mother that should news of the affair with Hippolytus be discovered, 'We'd be torn apart on the streets' (73), and the danger that their subjects only pose allegiance is alluded to when Phaedra challenges Hippolytus, 'Why don't you riot like everyone else?' (74). Hippolytus also notes the fewer number of presents received that year, together with an act of vandalism to his car, as 'token[s] of their contempt' (75).

Such feelings metamorphose into the mob of scene eight who burn down the palace once it has been learnt that Hippolytus stands accused of his stepmother's rape. On being told that the populace riot Hippolytus muses, 'Life at last' (90), while simultaneously realising, 'I'm doomed' (91). His encounter with the Priest in scene six confirms that he is seen as little more than a figurehead for the nation's morality: rather than live untruthfully Hippolytus decides to put into practice a credo which up until then he has only acknowledged privately, 'I've lived by honesty let me die by it' (95).

In Britain, *Phaedra's Love* and *Cleansed* have both gained reputations as 'problem plays', and are rarely performed. *Phaedra's Love* is Kane's least formally experimental play, and some believe that it contains inherent weaknesses of logic such as Hippolytus' rejection of Phaedra being likened to rape.[38] These problems can be accounted for in part by applying T. S. Eliot's idea of the *objective correlative* to the final scene. Eliot used the term in his well-known essay *Hamlet and His Problems* (1919), where he put forward the idea that the believability of a tragic action comes from the degree of emotional truthfulness that motivates it. *Phaedra's Love* is the only play by Kane in which this objective correlative is missing, and where a deliberately 'in-yer-face' sensibility dominates over a rational one. In essence, this comes down to Phaedra's action of suicide being sufficient cause to set in motion the excessive acts of violence against members of the family.

The incredulity of certain critics and audiences to its first production in 1996 at the Gate Theatre may have been exacerbated by the cramped playing space and close proximity of the actors to the audience – a reality only exaggerated by Kane's decision to place the actors involved in the mob scene directly amongst the audience, thereby removing the distancing barrier of the stage.

Sarah Kane has called *Phaedra's Love* 'a comedy',[39] and it is difficult to ascertain how seriously we are meant to take certain elements of the final cataclysmic scene. Some have seen the ending as a failure in terms of its politics in that it is left undisclosed whether the monarchy is overthrown and a new power structure established in its place.[40] However, a key feature of *Phaedra's Love* comes from the use of grotesque humour to shape its politics. The mob, after all, have come with their children *and barbecue sets* (98) to enjoy the public execution of a royal prince. Theseus disguised in the crowd also throws out inflammatory remarks borrowed from the clichés of tabloid news reporting, that the mob all too readily embrace, 'String him up, they should/Parasites . . . Pig-shit thick, the lot of them' (99). The mob also uses the illogical blanket justification for vigilantism in modern life: 'Don't deserve to live. I've got kids' (100). In stark contrast to the clownish and easily malleable crowd, Hippolytus ends his life with a strange sort of dignity, dying as he lived through a philosophy of absolute honesty.

Skin

Although made as a short ten-minute film, perhaps *Skin* should be seen as Kane's second play, after *Blasted*. This is substantiated by its inclusion in the posthumously published volume, *Sarah Kane: Complete Plays*. *Skin* certainly contains themes and imagery familiar to Kane's theatre work.

The film is about Billy, a young skinhead, who joins in a brutal racist attack on a mixed-race wedding party, but then finds himself drawn to Marcia, a black woman whose flat is visible from Billy's window. He visits Marcia, the couple have sex, she carves her name on his back, but finally rejects him. Billy unsuccessfully takes an overdose but is saved by his black neighbour.

Skin was completed over the summer of 1995, the same year *Blasted* premiered at the Royal Court. It was directed by Vincent O'Connell, a friend Kane had known since adolescence who is best known for his screenplay about football hooliganism, *I.D.* (1995). *Skin* formed part of a series of shorts entitled *Short and Curlies* made by Channel 4/British Screen, and was broadcast on Channel 4 television on 17 June 1997. The controversial subject matter of the film can be gauged by the fact that its original screening time of 9.40 p.m. was changed to 11.35 p.m.

Skin is concerned with themes of identity and race. Billy, its chief protagonist, at first seems to be an acolyte of both skinhead culture and right wing ideology with the swastika that he draws on his fist. Yet the extent of Billy's involvement and commitment to fascism is never entirely convincing. These doubts are highlighted through small instances such as the elaborate and unnecessary ritual of applying both shampoo and conditioner 'to his almost bald head' (250) and, in a scene reminiscent of Cate's disgust at the two English breakfasts Ian orders in *Blasted* (35), Billy refuses to share any of the gang's meal of sausages and bacon (251).

Such behaviour suggests an individual who is a recent convert or an outsider to the group. Billy's mother calls her son 'William', and in her answerphone message states, 'I'm very worried about you' (250). The extent to which Billy wholeheartedly engages with race hatred is also questioned throughout the film. On one occasion he is perturbed at seeing a small mixed race boy staring at him from outside the café holding the same 'cuddly polar bear' (252) that we have seen at the foot of his bed in scene one; and his readiness to visit the black woman Marcia also seems to be motivated for reasons other than racism.

Surface identity, especially the iconographies of Englishness and fascism, informs the film. This includes the Union Jack tattoos and swastika that Billy draws on his fist (which he kisses during the wedding fight), to Billy's change from 'tight blue jeans, white tee-shirt, red braces and cherry red docs' (256) to 'black baggy jeans, tee-shirt and a black denim jacket' (257) when going to visit Marcia. It is significant that Kath, who appears to share the flat with Marcia, is also a white skinhead and is dressed in an exact replica of Billy's discarded clothes (257).

Billy's encounter with Marcia signals a further change of identity. She attempts to both physically erase external signs of his racism through scrubbing away the tattoos and swastika with bleach, while simultaneously imposing her own identity as a black woman. This extends from 'cutting her name into . . . [Billy's] back with a stanley knife' (262) to Billy dressing in Marcia's clothes (263). The reason behind these cruelties appears to be Marcia's desire to make Billy acknowledge his own acts of violence and racism. For instance, in one sequence we see Marcia 'slapping him around the head and face hard' and repeating like a mantra, 'What's it like?' (261).

Yet their relationship is complex. Marcia represents more than a vengeful dominatrix. Her acts of violence against Billy are followed by acts of contrition: 'she cries silently, and licks away the blood' (262) reads one direction in the script. Moreover, the relationship is never as one-sided as it may at first seem. While Billy is ultimately rendered passive, during one instance when he is 'licking, kissing and smelling MARCIA'S skin', her 'hand [is] stuffed in her mouth to stop her making any noise' (261).

Skin is probably Kane's most 'realistic' work in that it seems to overtly address issues of race politics. As *Blasted* begins in Leeds, *Skin* is set in Brixton, London. Both play and film look at the consequences of the extreme right-wing ideologies that Ian and Billy embrace. Although the meeting between Billy and Marcia/Ian and the Soldier privilege issues of personal identity and salvation over social commentary, *Skin* does address questions of miscegenation with mixed-race marriage and the figure of the boy. Moreover, the closing image of Billy's black neighbour intervening to prevent his suicide seems to advocate a message of racial integration. Such affirmative endings are notably absent in the remainder of Kane's work for theatre.

Cleansed

Kane returned to the Royal Court with her third play *Cleansed*, in April 1998. Parts of this twenty-scene drama predate *Blasted*, and it had taken Kane over three years to complete. *Cleansed* marked a renewal of the partnership between Kane and director James Macdonald.

The play is set in a former university that seems to function as a hybrid prison/hospital. Its main protagonist is a young woman called Grace who pursues an obsessive and incestuous love for her dead brother Graham, a former drug addict and inmate of the institution. During a visit to reclaim her brother's clothes Grace submits herself to Tinker, an ambiguous figure who seems to have control over the lives of the other inmates. Grace undergoes torture, but she is also reunited with her brother's ghostly presence and eventually makes love to him. She submits herself to Tinker's crude surgery by which, through a penis transplant, she is made to parody her brother.

Other scenes in *Cleansed* show relationships between the inmates. One of these concerns two homosexual men, Carl and Rod, whose love Tinker tests under torture. A young man, Robin, falls in love with Grace after she has taught him to read and count. Tinker also seems to find love with a woman who formerly danced for him inside a peephole booth. However, the play ends with Grace still incarcerated in the institution and subsumed by her brother's identity.

As mentioned, the setting of *Cleansed* takes place within a former university. Stuart McQuarrie, who played the character of Tinker in the Royal Court production, has commented that locations in the play had undergone a reversal of function, reminiscent of the way in which football stadiums and schools have been transformed in repressive political regimes to places of imprisonment and torture.[41] This recalls one of the chief literary sources informing *Cleansed* – namely the linguistic device of Double-Speak and the various Ministries in George Orwell's novel *Nineteen Eighty-Four* (1949). Here, the Ministry of

Peace is really the Ministry of War, while the Ministry of Love is given over to inquisition and torture.

Like Kane's previous work, acts of physical brutality preoccupy *Cleansed*. Most of these revolve around the figure of Tinker, who seems to adopt the role of a moral experimenter, testing the boundaries to which love can survive betrayal and torture. Tinker either carries out or inaugurates a series of punishments that range from the ritualised dismemberment of Carl and murder of his lover Rod, to the torture of Grace under the guise of helping her to surgically resemble her dead brother Graham.

Although *Cleansed* is Kane's most violent play in terms of the number of staged acts, its main theme concerns the exploration of love. In *Blasted*, moments of kindness are suggested such as Cate feeding Ian, but they are rendered problematic by the stage direction, '*She finishes feeding* **Ian** *and sits apart from him*' (61). In *Cleansed*, scenes of cruelty are juxtaposed with those of tenderness in which love is shown to express itself even under the harshest of conditions. This includes moments such as the beating of Rod, and Carl's torture (116–118), followed by Grace performing a dance of love for her brother. Subsequently they make love, after which '*A sunflower bursts through the floor . . .*' (120).

Cleansed is also Kane's most overtly Shakespearian/Jacobean play.[42] Despite its dark subject matter, the play is reminiscent in theme and structure of Shakespeare's *A Midsummer Night's Dream* (c.1595) and *Twelfth Night* (c.1601). In these comedies, the principal characters are in love and, despite misunderstandings and obstacles, reconciliation eventually prevails through marriage. In *Cleansed*, things end rather differently. Grace is in love with her dead brother; Tinker loves Grace; Carl loves Rod; Robin loves Grace, while the unnamed Woman is in love with Tinker. By the end of the play Tinker seems to have found love with the Woman and Rod has reciprocated his love for Carl. However, in the interim Robin has committed suicide, Rod has been murdered and Carl has undergone ritual amputation of his hands, feet and tongue. Grace has also been given a double mastectomy and phalloplasty (from Carl's genitals) by Tinker in a bid to resemble her brother. Her reconciliation with Graham is a 'happy ending' predicated on a form of delusional psychosis.

Arguably, one of Kane's cruellest scenes is performed in *Cleansed*, when Robin is made to consume a whole box of chocolates that he has bought as a love token for Grace. While Kane has visited this territory before in *Blasted* by making the actor playing the Soldier consume two English breakfasts, in *Cleansed* the action is far more studied and deliberate in the cruelty it shows to actor and audience. That Kane sets out to nauseate at this point is substantiated by textual evidence. In the original 1998 play script, Tinker makes Robin eat twelve chocolates. In the rewrite, another layer of twelve chocolates is added. In fact, Kane sustains the effect by tricking the audience into thinking that the ordeal is over once the first layer of chocolates has been consumed. The stage directions read, '*Tinker takes the empty tray* [of chocolates] *out of the box*', but the spectator is then confronted with the revelation, '*there is another layer of chocolates underneath*' (140). The torture is then repeated until the entire box of chocolates has been eaten in front of the spectator.

This disturbing scene taps directly into Western culture's preoccupation between the consumption of food and the construction of selfhood. Seeing someone being tortured with a box of chocolates engages with contemporary debates over bingeing, anorexia/bulimia and obesity. The scene is also crucial in serving to illustrate an important feature of Sarah Kane's theatre – namely the relationship between emotion and analysis of stage action.

In the 2001 revival of *Blasted* at the Royal Court, assistant director Joe Hill-Gibbins recalled James Macdonald's view that experiencing the play involved a complex interaction between an emotional and speculative response, 'Kane wanted people to experience something emotionally before experiencing it intellectually. *Blasted* hits you so hard that you don't use your head until afterwards'.[43] The chocolate-eating scene in *Cleansed* serves to illustrate this process. For instance, when Robin wets himself and is made to clean the floor by Tinker, he uses the first object available to him – the chocolate box. This destruction of the object with which Robin had hoped to demonstrate his love for Grace is compounded by his previous consumption of the chocolates that were meant for her. This action under torture is reminiscent of an earlier scene (four) where Carl is made by Tinker to swallow his lover's ring as a gesture of forced betrayal. Robin is unsuccessful in mopping up his own urine with the chocolate box and moves on to destroy several of the books Grace had been teaching him to read from. Robin quickly realises the consequences of his actions as he '*looks at the books, distraught*' (141); this second act of betrayal is compounded by Tinker who makes Robin burn the remainder of the books. Grace appears, and her loss of identity through torture is shown by her complete indifference to the burning of her possessions. Instead, she warms her hands from the blaze and utters a refrain used by her brother – 'Lovely' (141).

Cleansed makes further significant moves away from formal constructions of realism that can be found in parts of *Blasted*, *Phaedra's Love* and *Skin*. James Macdonald commented, 'If you tried to stage *Cleansed* realistically you would burst a blood vessel . . . It would be unwatchable,'[44] and recounted a story concerning fellow director Peter Zadek's first German production of *Cleansed* in 1998, which decided initially to use live rats in scenes which call for their appearance:

> Having spent six months training them . . . Zadek had cut the poor rodents at the dress rehearsal. Apparently, the author had committed a serious error of dramaturgy – the brown rat is not actually capable of picking up a human foot. And the little bastards just wouldn't take direction.[45]

Despite *Phaedra's Love* appearing in the interim, many critics assumed *Cleansed* was the follow-up to *Blasted*. While the

Royal Court showed a commendable faith in the play by putting it on in the main house, both critical reaction and audience attendance were generally poor. While some acknowledged the power of its writing,[46] others saw it as 'portentous drivel, exquisitely dressed in designer chic'.[47]

Cleansed marked a significant departure from *Blasted* and *Phaedra's Love* in its move away from realism to a willingness to experiment with different types of dramatic form. An even more radical change of direction marked Kane's last two plays. In both, her predilection for testing methods of theatrical representation took a surprising new turn.

Towards a Poetic Drama: *Crave* and *4.48 Psychosis*

Crave not only prompted a radical change in style, but also marked a sea change in British critical opinion. Oddly, its experimental form involving rhythmic language, and absence of formal characterisation or stage action, failed to deter critics or audiences from appreciating the play. This may be explained in part by its many recognisable literary references, as well as the absence of staged acts of sex and violence that had attracted so much negative criticism in the past.

This is not to say that *Crave* or *4.48 Psychosis* are less intense experiences. By contrast, their power resides not in action but in language. This is particularly so in *Crave*, where its poetic structure, based exclusively around pace and rhythm, resists rational analysis.

Crave has four characters – A, B, C and M – but no stage directions. While the characters speak in turn, and occasionally seem to answer each other, there is no sense of traditional dialogue. Although their relationships with each other are fluid, as Ruby Cohn pointed out, each character has a coherent personality.[48] A says that he/she is a paedophile, C talks of experiencing abuse, M yearns for a child, and B wants to be seduced by an older woman. When each character speaks, they could be addressing one or more of the other characters. The exchanges between the two pairs seem to take place against two time scales: the relationship between B and M appears to be ongoing whereas there is the sense of a history between A and C. Yet this is certainly not constant throughout, and *Crave* is distinguished by the endless interpretations that can be given to the exchanges, depending on which character one imagines is being addressed.

In *Crave*, all the characters have been damaged by their relationships. The repetition of lines such as 'You're dead to me' and 'I feel nothing' articulate this pervading sense of despair. Certainly, Kane saw *Crave* as the bleakest of her plays because its characters have ceased to have faith in redemption through love and choose, instead, to embrace the void of a 'world without end' (200).

These elements of abuse, memory and yearning manifest themselves in the characters' frequent allusions to family. C, for instance, reveals, 'I told my mother, You're dead to me,' (155) and recalls an incident where they 'watched my father beat my mother with a walking stick' (179). M rebukes C by saying, 'Grow up and stop blaming mother,' (191) yet tells B, 'I could be your mother' (182). These contradictory feelings based around a need, fear and hatred of the family are illustrated by A's story of the child who hides bottles of milk as a way of coping with their parents' rows (185). This is set against the way characters frequently blur the boundaries between parental and sexual relationships. This can be seen in the mother/son dynamic between B and M that reveal the former's need 'to be seduced by an older woman' (158).

The four characters in *Crave* seem to be engaged on the same quest to find physical and emotional contact with each other, although ultimately the only connection that seems to be made in both *Crave* and *4.48 Psychosis* is through death. Both plays adopt a fragmentary style, and *4.48 Psychosis* also continues the hospital narrative from *Crave* (187–8).

Through their shared use of tone, both *Crave* and *4.48 Psychosis* give the impression of being intimate and personal plays – almost confessional in style. In the first British production of *Crave*, this was made apparent through choice of staging, with the protagonists seated in a manner reminiscent of TV confessional shows. Yet setting was at odds with content. In place of belligerent audiences, an introspective tone was established. Paul Taylor observed that the clash resulted in 'Jerry Springer meets T. S. Eliot'.[49] However, *Crave* privileges the confessional over the confrontational and asks the audience to interpret these two very different discourses.

In *4.48 Psychosis*, the five dialogues seem to closely resemble the exchanges between a doctor and patient, although in *Crave* this interpretation implies that the audience, cast in the role of listening psychiatrist/doctor, will interpret the play through careful analysis. Yet the speed of delivery and its emotional impact mean that *Crave* actively refuses to privilege any form of speculative response by the audience. Director Vicky Featherstone confirmed that this was a deliberate policy, in that it not only forced the audience to experience the play moment by moment through the senses, but also served to concentrate attention on the intrinsic rhythms of its exchanges.[50]

In *Crave*, fragmentary quotations taken from literary, religious and popular culture are embedded within the characters' own elliptical narratives. Additionally, these numerous literary and cultural fragments can stand alone as quotations and yet simultaneously transform themselves into a new context. So, for example, the well-known line from T. S. Eliot's *The Wasteland*, 'HURRY UP PLEASE IT'S TIME' (162) is a call for drinkers to leave the pub. In *Crave*, it is used to emphasise the ultimate nihilism that the protagonists seem to accept for themselves.

Crave and *4.48 Psychosis* also set out to explore the act of writing. While in *Crave* there is a lament – 'I hate these words that won't let me die . . . Expressing my pain without easing it' (184) – *4.48 Psychosis* dramatises the anxieties that afflict the creative mind. Here, one of the speakers fears that the effects of mental illness and the drugs used to treat it will destroy their creativity, 'How can I return to form/now my formal thought has gone?' (213). There are also overt displays of Kane's authorial voice which at times seem to pre-empt critics such as Peter Morris who showed scepticism over whether *4.48 Psychosis* constituted a performance text[51] – doubts that seem to be refuted with the short statement, 'just a word on the page and there is the drama' (213). There is even an engagement with her critics, in which a phrase from Alastair Macaulay's review of *Cleansed*, labelling Kane an 'expressionist nag',[52] is quoted and then answered with the line, 'They know nothing –/I have always walked free' (213).

Both plays share an exploration of abusive relationships, although *4.48 Psychosis* uses dramatic form to represent a mental state in which distinctions between reality and delusion have broken down. Caridad Svich commented on this disjunction with reference to the revival of the original Royal Court production when it toured America in 2004:

> Mental illness is not held up for view as a case study here; the audience is rather asked to enter the state of illness: to experience with artful distance the pain of thoughts fractured, seemingly divorced from the self.[53]

These last two plays tempt a biographical reading. This is one of the most frequent points of discussion on the main Sarah Kane website, where enthusiasts frequently attempt to make connections between Kane's life and work. This preoccupation stems from the circumstances of her death and is augmented by the fact that Kane occasionally acted in her own work, playing the roles of two suffering protagonists – Grace in *Cleansed* and C in *Crave*.

The biographical reading given to *4.48 Psychosis* performed fourteen months after her suicide and considered 'a dramatized suicide note'[54] is perhaps inevitable, although it is important to note that interview evidence shows Kane had begun work on *4.48 Psychosis* from at least January 1998 onwards – over a year before her death. Aleks Sierz pointed out that the play was a formal attempt at breaking up a performance text to describe the state of psychosis where the boundaries between selfhood and the outside world have disintegrated, rather than the personal account of a psychological condition.[55]

Nevertheless, it is undeniable that Kane's own death informed the first posthumous performances of *4.48 Psychosis*. This was made particularly explicit with the last lines of the play, 'please open the curtains' (245), after which the actors opened the shutters inside the small Theatre Upstairs letting in the evening sunlight, the sounds of traffic and people on the street outside. Speaking from personal experience as a member of the audience, the effect was similar to the closing of a funeral ritual. Here, the action seemed to produce a laying to rest of the dead person's spirit, and so allowed the audience to both re-evaluate and affirm their own lives through experiencing the play.

Kane on Kane: A Digest of Interviews and Journalism

All following extracts are from interviews recorded with Sarah Kane. Subsequent references will refer to either the name of the interviewer or wireless programme.

Benedict Nightingale, 'Disgusting Violence? Actually It's Quite a Peaceful Play', *Independent on Sunday*, 22 January 1995.

Clare Bayley, 'A Very Angry Young Woman', *Independent*, 23 January 1995.

Start the Week, broadcast on BBC Radio 4, 20 February 1995.

Graham Saunders, Interview with Sarah Kane, 12 June 1995.

David Benedict, 'What Sarah Did Next', *Independent*, 15 May 1996.

Natasha Langridge and Heidi Stephenson, *Rage and Reason: Women Playwrights on Playwriting* (London, 1997), pp. 129–35.

Rodolfo di Giammarco, Interview with Sarah Kane, 16 September 1997. Originally published in Graham Saunders, *'Love Me or Kill Me': Sarah Kane e il Teatro Degli Estremi* (trans.) Lino Belleggia (Rome, 2005), pp. 17–22.

James Christopher, Interview with Sarah Kane, London, October 1997.

Kate Stratton, 'Extreme Measures', *Time Out*, 25 March– 1 April 1998.

Claire Armitstead, 'No Pain, No Kane', *Guardian*, 29 April 1998.

Sarah Kane, 'Afterword to *Blasted*', in *Frontline Intelligence: New Plays for the Nineties* (London, 1994)

Sarah Kane, 'The Only Thing I Remember Is', *Guardian*,
13 August 1998.
——, 'Drama with Balls', *Guardian*, 20 August 1998.
Nils Tabert (ed.), 'Gespräch mit Sarah Kane', in *Playspotting:
Die Londoner Theaterszene der 90er* (Reinbeck, 1998),
pp. 8–21.
Caroline Egan, 'The Playwright's Playwright', *Guardian*,
21 September 1998.
Dan Rebellato, 'Brief Encounter Platform', Public Interview
with Kane, Royal Holloway, London, 3 November 1998.
http://www.rhul.ac.uk/drama/staff/rebellato_dan/index.html
Aleks Sierz, Interview with Sarah Kane, 4 January 1999.
——, Interview with Sarah Kane, 18 January 1999.
Johan Thielemans, 'Sarah Kane and Vicky Featherstone', in
Andrew McKinnon (ed.), *Rehearsing the Future: 4th
European Directors Forum – Strategies for the Emerging
Director in Europe* (London, 1999), Part 2: 'Voices',
pp. 9–15.

Influences

The specific influences for *Blasted* are early Pinter and early
Ibsen. I think that my main influences in reality are European
rather than English, and I lean towards non-theatre narratives:
the main ones are Kafka and Mikhail Bulgakov.[1] In reality, it is
very difficult to trace the history of a work or the history of a
writer, especially when that writer is you. In a way therefore I
don't really know what to say, except that if you can write
something worth half of a great tragedy or arrive near to
[Georg Büchner's] *Woyzeck* you would be very happy
(Giammarco, 1997).

[I] mainly [read] non-English stuff, except for Pinter, Barker
and Bond. It's mainly European literature. I think with everything I write there are usually a couple of books that I read
again and again when writing. With *Cleansed* it was *Woyzeck*,

Nineteen Eighty Four, Twelfth Night[2] and Strindberg's *The Ghost Sonata*.[3] *Blasted* was *King Lear* and *Waiting for Godot*.[4] It was strange with *Blasted* because for me there are three sections: the first one was very influenced by Ibsen; the second one by Brecht and the third one by Beckett.[5] *Phaedra's Love* was Brecht's *Baal*,[6] and Camus' *The Outsider*.[7] *Crave* was *The Wasteland*. And the new one [*4.48 Psychosis*] it's Artaud (Tabert, 1998).

Franz Kafka

Franz Kafka (1883–1924). German-speaking Czech writer, probably best known for novels such as The Trial *(1925) and short stories such as* The Metamorphosis *(1915). His writing is characterised by feelings of guilt and paranoia, expressed in sinister worlds where mundane reality exists uneasily within outlandish and often unexplained events.*

Kafka is a writer everybody thought was purely imaginative. But in retrospect, his works look like realism. And I think it's always that way – writers with the best imagination in retrospect look like realists. But at the time they look like they're completely off the wall, like with Orwell's *Nineteen Eighty-Four*. It's one of those books where nothing is ever specified; it never says this is what it is. But somehow you get it (Tabert, 1998).

Blasted and *King Lear*

In the section below, Kane refers to Edward Bond's Lear (1971), *a play that uses elements from Shakespeare's* King Lear *in order to look at the causes and nature of violence in contemporary society.*

There's always a risk rewriting an old story I suppose, especially when it's written by Shakespeare. I love *King Lear*. I really do. I don't have a problem with what Edward Bond does with it at all. The story of Lear is well known, but what Bond's *Lear* does is to completely rearrange it, and suddenly you see all that violence for what it really is all over again (Saunders, 1995).

The first two drafts of *Blasted* were written emotionally rather than intellectually. And although parts of it are very deliberate reworkings of *King Lear*, I didn't make that decision until some time into the process. Many of the thematic similarities were already there, but I didn't become consciously aware of them until the third draft, after someone suggested that I should re-read *King Lear*.

At the same time, I'd been reading Bill Buford's *Among the Thugs* which is about football violence. He joined up with a group of Manchester United supporters, and there was one particular incident in it, where there was an undercover policeman and he got into a row with someone from another firm. Someone just went up to him at a party, grabbed his head – sucked his eye out, bit it off and spat it on the floor. The policeman was unconscious as soon as the person did it. He was in such shock.[8]

And then I re-read *King Lear*, and I thought there's something about blinding that is really theatrically powerful. And given also that Ian was a tabloid journalist it was a kind of castration, because obviously if you're a reporter your eyes are actually your main organ. So I thought rather than have him castrated, which felt melodramatic, I could go for a more kind of metaphorical castration. The influence of *Lear* is also present in Ian's constant craving for death. I struggled with scene four for a long time. It was a void in the play – and I knew something went in there. I just couldn't think what. And then it dropped into my head. 'It's Ian's Dover Scene'. As straightforward as that. A blatant rewrite of Shakespeare[9] (Saunders, 1995).

I was doing a workshop on *Blasted* with this person who script-edited it and he said, 'Right I'm going to the toilet, and when I come back tell me what the title of the play is you're going to write', and I thought 'Oh, for fuck's sake'! I knew it was about someone who got drunk a lot, so he came out and I said, 'I'm going to call it *Blasted*.' It was only when I was into about the fourth draft that I suddenly thought, 'Of course, it's the blasted heath'![10] And by that time I was already reading *King Lear*, and it was beginning to act as an influence, but it was just sheerly coincidental; but once that happened I thought that maybe this is – I hate to say destiny – but I thought maybe there's some subconscious drive to rewrite that play. For me, *King Lear* is really a play about fatherhood (Saunders, 1995).

Georg Büchner's *Woyzeck*

Georg Büchner (1813–37). Dramatist, revolutionary and lecturer in comparative anatomy at the University of Zürich. Alongside Brecht, Büchner is generally seen as one of the great German playwrights in attempting to depict the 'modern' imagination.

Woyzeck is possibly an incomplete drama and was assembled after Büchner's death from his notes. As Kane pointed out, it is difficult to know in what order the scenes occur and structurally there is no formal development in terms of plot and characterisation. By the end of the play nothing is unified or resolved. Woyzeck also dispenses with notions of classical tragedy and the tragic hero, both of which dominated theatre at the time.

As Kane suggested, Woyzeck was significantly ahead of its time and came to be performed frequently in Germany after the First World War, often under the auspices of the artistic movement known as Expressionism. Moreover, Woyzeck also prefigures the late nineteenth-century movement of Naturalism in its exploration of the system of morality in society and its effect upon the individual.

It is easy to see why Woyzeck appealed to Kane. Its central protagonist's credo of absolute honesty brings about his suffering in a world where (like Cleansed) science has been corrupted, categories based on Christian notions of good and evil have broken down, and sexuality is depicted as violent and primal. Kane also directed a production of Woyzeck at the Gate Theatre, London in October 1997.

When I read *Woyzeck* for the first time I was about seventeen. I didn't understand it at all, but it had something that made me return to it. I believe the thing that fascinated me about *Woyzeck*, even if I didn't realize it was . . . that it was the only piece that I had ever read that was completely non-coherent and yet for me had the capacity to have a clear meaning. Although you can't say that there was a direct relationship between the reading of this text and the writing of *Blasted* there was certainly a direct relationship with the second part of the trilogy that was entitled *Cleansed*, for which my use of *Woyzeck* as a model was deliberate and conscious.[11] The thing I found really extraordinary about this piece, that I wanted to capture myself, was that for me the scenes were like balloons that in a way float above ground but at the same time are tied to the earth, rooted but floating (Giammarco, 1997).

Every version you read, the scenes are in a different order – the language is dreadful. With the exception of one production at the Other Place last year it's always been horribly fragmented and stilted.[12] You spend more time looking at the black out than looking at the scenes because they're so short. I wanted to do something that could be a more fluid piece of theatre, and so part of working out the order [of scenes] was to make the story more fluid without making it more linear which is quite a hard thing to do. It's not meant to be linear. It's the first time you have a play about people who have nothing. Even Jimmy Porter has articulacy, but Woyzeck has nothing at all. That doesn't happen again until [Edward Bond's] *Saved* over a hundred years later which is pretty remarkable. He [Woyzeck] isn't hollow at all – he just doesn't have any of the normal means to express himself, or better himself, or get anything that he wants. The only way in the end is violence. There's something about him which is almost like a clown and he's batted around by everyone. But that doesn't make him dramatically uninteresting.

Büchner died young, but he wrote one of the greatest plays ever written because first of all it's the first play about people who have nothing; also, that play simultaneously gives birth to Naturalism and Expressionism. It's hard to imagine how he did that. I suspect it was by accident like most really great work. In rehearsals we'd be reading something out and someone would say this was like Pinter or Brecht or Beckett – a complete range of playwrights who you would never normally put together. I may be wrong, but when I read it I thought Pinter must have read this many times.[13] People say Büchner was ahead of his time – he was ahead of our time as far as I'm concerned, which is why the play has never really been done very well (Christopher, 1997).

Cleansed is structurally based on *Woyzeck*, Büchner's play which I directed last year. It's the difference between plot and story. Story is what chronologically happens. The plot is the order in which the story is revealed. With *Blasted*, for example, the story and the plot are similar, in that eventually all of those things are revealed.

Anything remotely extraneous or explanatory is completely cut and all you get is those moments of high drama. What I was trying to do with *Cleansed* was a similar thing, but in a different way. I'd actually finished *Cleansed* when I directed *Woyzeck*, and I was playing around with all of the different versions. I moved them around and thought, 'When have I done this before'? And I remembered *Cleansed*, where I wrote all of the story lines – the Rod and Carl story; the Grace and Graham story; the Robin and Grace story; and the Tinker/stripper story separately (Rebellato, 1998).

Henrik Ibsen
Henrik Ibsen (1828–1906). Norwegian dramatist, often referred to as the father of twentieth-century European drama. His later naturalistic works expose the corruption of middle-class life. Ibsen's best-known plays include A Doll's House *(1879),* Ghosts *(1881) and* Hedda Gabler *(1890).*
I believe that what fascinates me about Ibsen is his attention to

detail; there are few holes in his texts. Personally it makes me aware of the holes in my texts, especially in terms of time scales. This probably comes from reading too much Shakespeare (Giammarco, 1997).

Crave and T. S. Eliot's *The Wasteland*

Eliot's poem, published in 1922, is one of the great works of Modernism and is generally seen as an expression of the mood of futility that arose throughout Europe in the aftermath of the First World War. Eliot included a set of notes at the end of the poem which outlined sources of the many literary and cultural allusions in the poem. Eliot has commented, 'I have sometimes thought of getting rid of these notes: but now they can never be unstuck. They have had almost greater popularity than the poem itself . . . my notes stimulated the wrong kind of interest among the seekers of sources . . . I regret having sent so many enquirers off on a wild goose chase after Tarot cards and the Holy Grail.'[14]

The play is very heavily influenced by *The Waste Land*, and I had a choice as to whether I wrote a set of notes to go with the play, to explain it. But what happened to T. S. Eliot, poor bastard – and I bet he regretted it forever – was that everyone became more interested in the notes than the poem; because how can you understand the poem without them? I really didn't want that to happen and I also knew that the notes section would actually be longer than the script, which would be just ridiculous. So it was a very simple choice; either I explain everything, which means going into enormous detail about my own life, which I didn't really want to do, or I explain nothing. And I thought I'll explain nothing and if no one likes it then who cares? (Rebellato, 1998).

Bertolt Brecht

Bertolt Brecht (1898–1956). German dramatist, director and theatre practitioner who did much to change the look, content and acting style of twentieth-century theatre. Through his drama, directing and theoretical writings Brecht developed what has generally come to be known as Epic Theatre. Brecht questioned past theatrical styles such as Naturalism, which attempted to create an illusion of realism on-stage. Epic Theatre promoted an engagement with political and social problems. Brecht's most well-known plays include Mother Courage and her Children *(1941),* The Caucasian Chalk Circle *(1948) and* The Resistible Rise of Arturo Ui *(1941).* The Life of Galileo *(English version 1943) is one of Brecht's most popular plays in translation. It concerns the conflict that the Renaissance scientist Galileo encountered when his challenge to the established view of the solar system came up against the religious authorities represented by the Inquisition.*

Galileo is one of my favourite plays. I've tried several times to work out why but I still don't know. I just read it and read it and read it, thinking how can you write a play about science which is somehow so extraordinary. I really do love it. And there is a connection with *Phaedra's Love* actually. Which is that thing about the relative value of truth; what's the point at which you say, 'I'll tell a lie here in order to save myself'? I think the relative value of whether the earth goes around the sun or does the sun go around the earth is really of no significance whatsoever. But somehow truth takes on a bigger significance (Tabert, 1998).

Samuel Beckett

Samuel Beckett (1906–89). Irish novelist and poet, although best known for plays such as Waiting for Godot *(1955),* Endgame *(1957) and* Not I *(1973). These spare dramas are often set in bleak worlds, where protagonists struggle to understand and accommodate their situation.*

Beckett I have always loved because he goes directly, absolutely to the heart in what he writes, and he does so in an emotional way; his language adapts incredibly to the expression of a particular emotion: yet in a way it also goes to the specifics of the situation. What I have tried to do with *Blasted* is to have

45

the detail of Ibsen in terms of situations, combined with Beckett's capacity to go straight to the heart with what he says (Giammarco, 1997).

I think my influences are quite obvious. Yes, Beckett, of course, but not particularly consciously, because I'm practically unconscious when I write, and I think once you're consciously influenced your voice becomes inauthentic. But I was steeped in Beckett so it's not surprising that *Blasted* ends with an image of a man with his head poking out of the floor with the rain pouring through the ceiling onto his head (60) (Sierz, 18 January 1999).

Jeremy Weller's Grassmarket Project
Theatre company set up by Jeremy Weller in 1990, which produces devised work, often based around autobiographical experiences of socially excluded groups. Kane's reference to Weller's 1998 production of Soldiers *concerned the personal experiences of combatants from both Northern Ireland and Bosnia; it was performed by a combination of actors and the soldiers themselves in a series of monologues. Prior to her death there were plans for Kane and Weller to collaborate on a joint project.*

Earlier this year, I was asked by *Time Out* to list the best ten shows of the past 30 years . . . Number one was Jeremy Weller's 1992 Edinburgh Grassmarket Project, *Mad*. (Second was a live sex show in Amsterdam about a witch sucking the Grim Reaper's cock.) *Mad*, a devised play with professional and non-professional actors who all had first-hand experience of mental illness, remains the only piece of theatre to have changed my life and is one of many reasons why [The] Edinburgh [Festival] is so important to me.

Weller's latest play, *Soldiers*, which examines the experience of men who have killed, bears the hallmarks of the Grassmarket Project – raw, emotional and authentic, it dragged me through a nightmare to make me happy to be awake again.

I felt sick afterwards hearing people say the Project's not as good as it used to be. I'm too young to remember the early days of the Fringe, though I'm told it's looking threadbare 25 years on. However, theatre exists in the moment of performance and then disappears. Who's to say that if I saw *Mad* now, I would still be devastated in the way I was at 21? Perhaps the power of that sex show in Amsterdam was more to do with the grass I was smoking than the stark images thrown together as an excuse to watch people fuck. It's impossible to say.

Theatre has no memory, which makes it the most existential of the arts. No doubt that is why I keep coming back, in the hope that someone in a dark room somewhere will show me an image that burns itself into my mind, leaving a mark more permanent than the moment itself (Kane, 'The Only Thing I Remember is', 1998).

It [*Mad*] was a very unusual piece of theatre because it was totally experiential as opposed to speculatory. As an audience member, I was taken to a place of extreme mental discomfort and distress and then popped out the other end. What I did not do was sit in the theatre considering as an intellectual conceit what it might be like to be mentally ill. It was a bit like being given a vaccine. I was mildly ill for a few days afterwards but that jab of sickness protected me from a far more serious illness later in life. *Mad* took me to hell, and the night I saw it I made a decision about the kind of theatre I wanted to make – experiential (Sierz, 4 January 1999).

Edward Bond
Edward Bond (b. 1934). One of the most influential post-war British dramatists. Like Blasted, *his play* Saved *(1965) caused a storm of protest – principally over a scene where a baby in a pram is stoned to death by a gang of youths.*
The first draft of *Blasted* was dreadful – it was full of huge dense monologues about characters' backgrounds, every feeling was stated, every thought spoken. A friend read it and

didn't say very much, but he gave me a copy of *Saved*, which I'd read years before but read again in 1993. And that really was where I learned to write dialogue. At first I thought Bond's approach would be of no use to me – I wanted my characters to be articulate and precise. But of course, if each character can only say nine or ten words at a time, they become incredibly articulate and precise. When I didn't let Ian elaborate on his racism, he just started to spill invective – it was a level of racism and violence that terrified me. Suddenly there was something happening that challenged me emotionally rather than reassured me intellectually.

I think there are only three or four lines in the first draft that made it through to the final one. But that first draft stood me in good stead. I knew just about everything I could know about these characters. Having brought it all to the surface, the job of the later drafts was to bury it again, make it felt rather than spoken (Sierz, 18 January 1999).

When I read *Saved*, I was deeply shocked by the baby being stoned. But then I thought there isn't anything you can't represent on stage. If you're saying you can't represent something, you are saying you can't talk about it, you're denying its existence, and that's an extraordinarily ignorant thing to do (Bayley, 1995).

Howard Barker

Howard Barker (b. 1946). British dramatist whose later work is often set in loose historical/mythical periods. He employs a form that is darkly poetic, non-realistic and frequently inhabits the extremes of sexual and violent passion.

I spent the first two years at Bristol [University] avoiding the department as much as I could. I acted and directed and wrote which I thought was much more important and interesting than anything I was actually supposed to be doing. In my first term I played Bradshaw in Howard Barker's *Victory*, which was an unusually brilliant experience.[15] Barker's control of lan-

guage is just extraordinary and I think I loved him all the m
because none of the teaching staff seemed to share my enthusi-
asm (Sierz, 4 January 1999).

In a few hundred years Howard will be like Shakespeare. No
one will really understand what Howard Barker's done until
he's been dead for a long time (Christopher, 1997).

Martin Crimp
Martin Crimp (b. 1956). British dramatist. His play Attempts on
Her Life *(1997) was a formal influence on* Crave. *See GS, pp.
111, 132 and Aleks Sierz,* The Theatre of Martin Crimp, *p.169.*
Martin Crimp is one of a small number of living dramatists
whose plays inspire me to push my own work in new directions. A lot of attention is focused on the more fashionable
and inaccurately named New Brutalists[16] because it's possible
to sensationalize the content of their plays, but for sheer qual-
ity of writing I think Martin is one of the best. He's remorse-
lessly unsentimental and has some very hard edges. His work
doesn't scream for attention, but he's one of the few genuine
formal innovators writing for the stage. He's constantly refin-
ing his language to find more accurate theatrical expression,
marrying rhythm and skill with real beauty. His precision
compels (Egan, 1998).

Blasted

Origins
Kane's accounts of the day she started writing Blasted *vary in
terms of dates, although the impetus of the siege of Srebrenica
remains constant. This culminated in one of the most well-doc-
umented atrocities of the conflict, where over the summer of
1995 Serbian forces massacred an estimated seven thousand
Muslim men.*
The day I started writing it was in 1992 when Srebrenica was
under siege, and I was getting more and more depressed having

been reading about what was happening in Bosnia during the previous two years, and then seeing all this footage on television. And there was a woman who looked directly at the camera, who looked about seventy years old; and her face was lined and grey – she was just crying her eyes out. And she just looked at the camera and said, 'Please, please help us. We don't know what to do, please help us', and I just sat there crying watching it; and it wasn't even so much a sense of helplessness, as just seeing such extreme pain. And I don't think it was conscious, but I think I started to want to write about that pain. That was probably when I had the idea that I wanted a soldier in it (Saunders, 1995).

I started writing *Blasted* in March 1993. I was twenty-two. Originally, I was writing a play about two people in a hotel room, in which the older man rapes the younger woman. At some point during the first couple of weeks writing, I switched on the television. Srebrenica was under siege. I was suddenly completely disinterested in the play I was writing. What I wanted to write about was what I'd just seen on TV. It gave me a dilemma – did I abandon my play even though I'd written one scene I thought was really good in order to move on to a subject I thought was more pressing? Slowly it occurred to me that the play I was writing was about this. It was about violence, about rape, and it was about these things happening between people who know each other and ostensibly love each other (Sierz, 18 January 1999).

Reception
I still think the highlight of my working life was the first preview. There were eight people in the audience: me, the director, my agent, a couple of friends. By the end, the other three people had walked out, but I didn't care. There was just something miraculous about sitting in an empty theatre watching my play. I had no idea what was going to happen after that. It was ninety-nine per cent great. Any twenty-three year old writer in

the country would be delighted to be singled out for a 'reputation' (Stratton, 1998).

I wasn't at all aware that *Blasted* would scandalize anyone. At
the time I wrote it, I didn't even expect it to be produced. I was
still a student when I started it. The most I could hope for was
a student production or maybe a production in a pub theatre if
I could get the money together. I certainly wasn't thinking far
enough ahead to imagine reviews.

Personally, I think it is a shocking play, but only in the sense
that falling down the stairs is shocking – it's painful and it
makes you aware of your fragility, but one doesn't tend to be
morally outraged about falling down the stairs (Sierz, 18
January 1999).

I think that the shock came from the press. It wasn't from audiences, and I think that's a point that has to be made. It was a
kind of self-perpetuating hysteria amongst journalists which
wasn't really shared by audiences. It did have walkouts around
about eyeball-munching time, that's fairly inevitable. However,
there wasn't a mass complaint from audiences. It was entirely
from the press, and I think that it's to do with the failure of the
critical establishment in this country to develop a satisfactory
critical language with which to talk about the plays . . . What
Blasted got – almost without exception – was a list of atrocities
as if this somehow was a value judgement on the play. And it is
what most theatre reviews are – a kind of synopsis of what
happens and then a short note at the end saying whether or not
this story was pleasing to the critic (*Start the Week*, 1995).

A lot of people in the building [The Royal Court] didn't want
to do [*Blasted*], they were a bit embarrassed about it, so they
put it into a spot just after Christmas when no one was going
to the theatre, and hopefully no one would notice it. What usually happens in the Theatre Upstairs is that they have two press
nights – because if you have one then every single seat is full of

press and it's completely unbearable. So you have two; then you have a slightly mixed audience on both nights. Because everyone was a bit haphazard at the Court at that time, they failed to notice that there was a major press night on at another theatre – the Almeida in London – so the critics were all coming on the same night.[17]

I was sitting at the back with a friend and I looked around and realized that the director was somewhere near the front and nearly everyone else was a critic. I think there were about three other women in the audience; everyone else was a middle-aged, white, middle-class man – most of them had plaid jackets on! It was literally only at that point that I realized that the character in my play was a middle-aged, male journalist, who not only rapes his own girlfriend but is then raped and mutilated himself. And it suddenly only then occurred to me that they weren't going to like it – it genuinely hadn't occurred to me! I thought they're going to love it! The next morning there was complete chaos; my agent couldn't call me – there were tabloid journalists running around the Royal Court. A lot of it passed me by at the time. My father's a tabloid journalist and he very kindly didn't give my address to any other tabloid journalists – they never caught up with me.

Because the dramatic form hadn't happened before, no one knew what to say. Michael Billington couldn't say, 'This is a nice bit of social realism – I can talk about this.' He couldn't say, 'It's Surrealism and I don't like that, therefore don't go and see it'. So what he could say was, 'Clearly this writer is mentally ill and she should be locked away'.[18] The *Daily Mail* did actually suggest that the money spent on the play should be spent on getting me some therapy. I agree, but that's clearly not the point [*Laughs*]! But I genuinely think it's because if they don't have a clear framework within which to locate the play they can't talk about it; so they have to talk about other things – such as the writer's personal life. Once it got picked up as a news story, it was no longer the people who had seen it who were actually writing about it. It was people like my father –

tabloid hacks – who if they don't know the facts make them up, because that's what their job is (Rebellato, 1998).

The week the play opened there was an earthquake in Japan in which thousands of people died, and in this country a fifteen-year-old girl had been raped and murdered in a wood.[19] But *Blasted* got more coverage in some newspapers than either of these events. And I'm not only talking about the tabloids. Of course it was surprising, and no one ever expects such a response (and if they do then they don't get it), but a lot of it passed me by.

I think it's important not to confuse press with audience. There was media outrage, but it was never a public outcry. And, as for whether or not the press response was to do with gender, I'm not sure. The explanation clearly can't be applied to Edward Bond or Howard Brenton whose plays provoked similar hostility (Langridge and Stephenson, 1997).

One of the disappointing things about *Blasted* was that no one could come and see it fresh any more because everyone had read about it, but it did mean that when I was watching it and people got up and walked out, there was part of me that thought, 'Why'd you come? You're really going to get offended by a man raping another man? You knew it was going to happen'! We had one man who walked out twenty seconds before the end, just as the rain started falling on Ian's face, and I thought, 'Well, you've obviously found nothing to walk out about – you realise it's about to end, so you're going' (Saunders, 1995).

The press outcry at the images presented wasn't outrage at the idea of such a thing actually happening, but about being asked to consider the idea when viewing that imagery. The shock wasn't about the content, not even about the shock of the new, but about the familiar being arranged in such a way that it could be seen afresh. The press was screaming about cannibalism live on stage, but of course audiences weren't looking at actual atrocities, but at an imaginative response to them in an odd theatrical form, apparently broken-backed and schizophrenic, which presented material without comment and asked the audience to craft their own response. The representation of violence caused more anger than actual violence. While the corpse of Yugoslavia was rotting on our doorstep, the press chose to get angry, not about the corpse, but about the cultural event that drew attention to it. That doesn't surprise me. Of course the press wished to deny that what happened in Central Europe has anything to do with us, of course they don't want us to be aware of the extent of the social sickness we're suffering from – the moment they acknowledge it, the ground opens up to swallow them. They celebrate the end of the Cold War then rapidly turn to sex scandals (which sell more papers) and all that has been done to secure our future as a species is the reduction of the overkill factor (Langridge and Stephenson, 1997).

The Profession of Journalism

I thought he [Ian] needed a job I know really well. My father's a tabloid journalist and the type of story Ian narrates I've heard my father do that so many times. Both the story that Ian dictates and the one he reads are actually straight from *The Sun*.[20] They're not fictional at all. I just changed the names and the places and I think added a couple of details and took a couple of things out – just because I wanted to make them slightly different, but I did want them to be the real thing. But Ian isn't my father. I do want to stress this! (Saunders, 1995)

I grew up with tabloid journalists so I knew what it was like. Whether the press say you're depraved or a genius, it makes no difference. It doesn't make the job of sitting down and writing any easier or any harder. It's always as hard as it is and that's that. It's only relevant to theatre in terms of selling tickets (Benedict, 1996).

The Character of Ian

The person I based Ian on was a man I knew a long time ago: very violent and very racist, sexist, homophobic – really unpleasant. He was going around with this whole mass of rage about all sorts of things which he directed towards women, but was also equally directed at female identified men, i.e. poofs basically (Saunders, 1995).

I could see that other people would say that Ian was a bastard, and I knew they would. But I think that he's extremely funny. The reason that I wrote his character was because of this terrible dilemma that was thrown up for me, with a man that I knew was dying of lung cancer. He was extremely funny, but started telling me the most appalling racist jokes I'd ever heard in my life. I was completely torn, because they were very funny and I'd not heard them before. I thought he was awful and I was glad he was dying. And it was because he was dying of lung cancer that I thought this poor man is going to be dead and he probably wouldn't be saying this. And it set up all kinds of turmoil in me (Rebellato, 1998).

In one interview Kane was asked a question whether she thought Ian was redeemed or punished by the end of the play. Ian is deified in a way I didn't realize until I saw the play performed for the first time. I wasn't around for the technical rehearsal because they said, 'Don't come in. You'll get bored and frustrated.' However, I went in for the technical run later on in the day. And when I watched the blood being washed away by the rain I saw how Christ-like the image is – which isn't to say that Ian isn't punished: he is of course, he dies, and he finds that the thing he's ridiculed – life after death – really does exist. And that life is worse than where he was before. It really is hell (Saunders, 1995).

In the same interview, Kane is asked about the nature of the relationship between Ian and the Soldier, and whether they are perhaps one and the same.

I suppose there is some sort of culpability implied because the Soldier is English, and he is a kind of personification of Ian's psyche in some sense; and it was a very deliberate thing. I thought that the person who comes crashing through the door actually has to make Ian look like a baby in terms of violence – and I think that's successful.

It's difficult, because when you look at what Ian does to Cate it's utterly appalling. And you think, 'I can't imagine anything worse', and then something worse happens. I find it very hard to say, 'God, what a horrible thing to do', even with Ian. In some sense, he's acted upon as much as he acts upon Cate. In a sense he's acted upon by his own nature – it's this thing rotting him from the inside which he feeds (Saunders, 1995).

Scene Five of *Blasted*

Here, blinded and left alone, Ian moves through a series of bizarre actions that include masturbating, strangling himself, laughing hysterically, having a nightmare, crying and hugging the body of the dead soldier for comfort. The actions are interspersed with stage directions that simply indicate darkness and light. The section culminates with Ian removing the infant that Cate had previously buried under the floorboards, and eating the corpse.

I actually thought that in terms of the [first Royal Court] production it was one of the least successful parts, but in terms of the writing it's one of the most successful parts of the play.

Whenever I read it I think, 'I'm really proud of this bit of writing.' It brought out a thing I hadn't thought about when I articulated it to the director, and he hadn't thought of it either. Cate says earlier on, 'Fate, see. You're not meant to do it. God,' and Ian says 'The cunt' (57). Now I think that's hilarious, but nobody else did! When Ian's masturbating and repeating the words 'Cunt, cunt, cunt, cunt' (59), it was really interesting because Pip Donaghy [the actor who played Ian] was looking up and it looked like he was praying, and I thought that's really interesting – it sets off all kinds of resonances about that thing of God being a cunt: and it was completely unconscious. None of us had planned it at all, but I thought that was where the production takes over, which is good because it should start setting up its own resonances.

In that scene Ian gets as low as he can get – he really does. But for me, it got to the point where I didn't know what words to use any more, and it was a complete breakdown of language. I thought I'm going to have to do this purely through image, which I'm happier doing anyway.

Ian's got to reach a point where he dies and he's in hell, and when he comes back he realizes he's just where he was before – he's dead. If that's going to be a moment of the most extreme horror then he has to get as low as he can get. And I thought I'll just take basic things, like eating, wanking and shitting and see how awful they can be when you're really unhappy – which is pretty awful.

The scene where Ian's masturbating started off as a joke. I was talking with a bloke who's a really close friend, and we were talking about the differences between men's and women's sexual fantasies. He said, 'It seems to me that women's sexual fantasies are like eighteenth-century novels. There's all this stuff around it, but there's never actually any sex. The fantasy is about the build-up and the restraint, and the fact that it doesn't happen.' And then I said, 'So what are men's sexual fantasies like'? He thought for a while, and I said, 'They're just basically cunt aren't they'? (Saunders, 1995)

The Character of Cate

I seem to have a completely different take to the rest of the world, which is I don't think Cate is simple. Cate constantly surprises me. She has this very idealized image of what sex should be, but it's not from a position of naiveté – she does actually have sex. She's slept with Ian before. She's had other boyfriends. She's going out with this bloke called Shaun. All right, she hasn't slept with him, but she's going to. I just don't see her as simple. I see her as possibly the most intelligent of them all.

The thing that stops Cate being a stereotype are those surprising things. She has sex with people which you don't expect, and I think everything is grounded specifically. I don't think there's any aspect of her supposed simpleness which isn't grounded. It might have been an unconscious thing because I was reading a lot of Shakespeare at the time, and I also read *Waiting for Godot*. Okay, Vladimir and Estragon aren't fools, but they're clowns who are capable of massive insight (Saunders, 1995).

Yes, I think Cate's very fucking stupid. What's she doing in that hotel room in the first place? Of course, she's going to get raped, and it's utterly tragic that this happens to her. I did have nights during rehearsals of *Blasted* when I would go home and cry and say, 'How could I create such a beautiful woman in order for her to be so abused'? I really did feel a bit sick and depraved. Part of that was to do with the fact that there was no sort of overwhelming sense that Cate came out on top. Had there been I'm sure I would have felt completely exonerated. But I didn't – and I don't think in the end these people do come out on top (Rebellato, 1998).

Her honesty . . .
It was such an annoying moment for me with the [1996] production of *Blasted* in Hamburg when Ian asks Cate, 'You ever had a fuck with a woman'? (19) – and they cut her saying no. It's a tiny detail, but for me it's important because again she is completely and utterly honest – up until when she finds the gun and Ian asks whether she's got it, and again she says no (56). Until then she does not tell a lie. And it's similar with Phaedra: she's actually very in touch with herself about what she wants, and she pursues it completely honestly – to the point where she's prepared to die for it. When I wrote *Blasted* I thought it was the most honest thing I could write, and yet

what I got accused of is cynicism which is the opposite of honesty (Tabert, 1998).

Her fits . . .
I knew someone who had *petit mal*,[21] and it was one of the
most disturbing things I've ever seen because it was almost
exactly what happened with Cate in *Blasted*. I obviously
changed it to make the scenes more theatrically interesting, but
my friend's fits took this odd form. First of all she would stare
at me and I would say, 'why are you staring at me?' And then
I'd realize that she'd gone completely, and then she'd pass out
and I'd think she was pissing me about. Then she'd suddenly sit
up and say something of great profundity – or banality,
depending on how you looked at it. It was really worrying. I
remember, it was years and years ago: she suddenly sat up and
said to me, 'you're in danger.'[22] And I said, 'what are you talking about?' She replied, 'don't go there.' I was saying, 'don't go
where? Where mustn't I go?' And she started stuttering on the
letter b. Eventually she said, 'Brisbane.' I didn't pay attention
to what she said, then last year I was in Australia. I got off my
head on the 'plane, and during the trip it made a stop-over to
change planes. In the airport I was stopped by two policemen
who opened everything I had looking for drugs, and it was only
two days later that I realized I'd been in Brisbane. It never
occurred to me that I'd go there. Was it sheer coincidence, or is
there something in what happened? I can't imagine that happening with a bloke. Why is that? (Saunders, 1995).

The Theme of Christianity
*Here Kane is asked about the debate that seems to be set up in
scene four where Cate tries to deter Ian from committing suicide
because 'God wouldn't like it.' Ian replies, 'No God. No Father
Christmas. No fairies. No Narnia. No fucking nothing' (55).*
Well, it's interesting because in a way I didn't consciously set up
that debate. But there is a debate I constantly have with myself
because I was brought up as a Christian, and for the first sixteen

59

years of my life I was absolutely convinced that there was a God. I belonged to a Charismatic Christian church which was very much focused on the Second Coming. I was convinced that I would never die. I seriously believed that Jesus was going to come again in my lifetime and that I wouldn't have to die. So, when I got to about eighteen or nineteen it suddenly hit me that the thing I should have been dealing with from the age of six – my own mortality – I hadn't dealt with at all. So, there is a constant debate in my head about really not wanting to die; being terrified of it, and also having this constant thing that you can't really shake off if you've believed it that hard and that long as a child – that there is a God, and somehow I'm going to be saved. So, I suppose in a way that debate in *Blasted* is a split in my personality and intellect about how I feel about that issue. And it was only afterwards that I thought, 'Oh yes, that's me and that's me', at different points in the dialogue. I don't know which side the play comes down on at all. I don't think it does, because I don't know. I've no idea (Saunders, 1995).

The Morality of *Blasted*
When Blasted *was first published in the anthology* Frontline Intelligence 2, *Kane included the following short afterword.*
Blasted now exists independently of me – as it should do – and to attempt to sum up its genesis and meaning in a few paragraphs would be futile and of only passing interest. If a play is good, it breathes its own air and has a life and voice of its own. What you take that voice to be saying is no concern of mine. It is what it is. Take it or leave it (Sarah Kane, 1994).

In the sections below Kane expands on this point in more detail.
The one thing I don't think is the responsibility of playwrights is telling people what to think about the play afterwards. I adore Edward Bond's writing and I think that the forewords and afterwords he writes are brilliant, but there's no point in me trying to do that because I can't do it – it's not what I am.

And also I don't know what the play is about necessarily. I think it's up to other people to tell me. It's not a case of not wanting to take more responsibility for what I've created, because for me the responsibility is taken in the act of writing it, and you make the decisions as you go along – that's when you take responsibility. There was so much debate about the morality of *Blasted* and its politics – well there wasn't actually enough debate; it was all just a kind of panic in the press about it. One of the major criticisms was 'Sarah Kane doesn't know what she thinks.' For me, the job of an artist is someone who asks questions, and a politician is someone who pretends to know the answers. And a bad artist is someone who's actually a politician. And I think what can I do other than say, 'Well there's this problem', and look at some of the aspects of the problem and let people make up their own minds (Saunders, 1995).

I think that a lot of the people who have defended me over *Blasted* have said that it's a deeply moral play. I use the word 'peaceful' because I don't think *Blasted* is a moral play. I think it's amoral and I think that is one of the reasons people got terribly upset because there isn't a very defined moral framework within which to place yourself and assess your own morality – or distance yourself from the material. I think there's a great deal of moral manoeuvre in the play and that's probably one of the distressing things. I suppose that ultimately it's not only about social breakdown – it's about the breakdown of human nature itself (*Start the Week*, 1995).

The play was about a crisis of living. How do we continue to live when life becomes so painful, so unbearable? *Blasted* really is a hopeful play, because the characters do continue to scrape a life out of the ruins. There's now a very famous photograph of a woman hanging by her neck from a tree. That's lack of hope. That's shocking. My plays are only a shadowy representation of a reality that is far harder to stomach. It's easier to get upset about the representation than it is about the reality it comes from because it's easier to do something about a play – ban it, censor it, take away the theatre's Arts Council subsidy – but what can you do about that woman in the woods? Take away her funding? (Sierz, 18 January 1999).

There is an attitude that certain things could not happen here [the UK]. Yet there's the same amount of abuse and corruption in Essex as anywhere else, and that's what I want to blow open. Just because there hasn't been a civil war in England for a very long time doesn't mean that what is happening in Bosnia doesn't affect us (Bayley, 1995).

The Issue of Rape

I read Andrea Dworkin when I was at Bristol [University] as an undergraduate.[23] I was just so horrified by it. I thought how can someone be filled with such hatred – be so blind and this politically stupid? It's interesting about what kind of moral judgement we can make about sexual fantasy. I do always think that in fantasy anything goes, and I do think that it's completely possible to spend your entire life fantasizing about killing and raping people, but actually have no desire to do that in reality at all. But I think my whole problem with Andrea Dworkin is that she assumes that people aren't intelligent enough to know the difference between fantasy and reality. And I think that most of the time people who are looking at pornography are completely aware that it's a construct, and that's part of what gets them off. It's the fact that it's not real.

There's also the whole other area of hardcore porn. When I first arrived in Birmingham [in October 1992 to start an MA in Playwriting], I got the mail from this person who had been living there before me, who'd been on a mailing list for hardcore porn but hadn't bothered to cancel it. So I kept getting all this stuff addressed to 'The Occupier' which I always opened. There was one particular image that I've never managed to get rid of which was a woman being fucked by a horse whilst having her head chopped off. Now, I kept looking at it and thinking that it looked completely real – but probably it wasn't. So does it matter whether it's real or not? And of course it does, because if it's real there's somebody who's dead who shouldn't be dead. It really did horrify me. I've always tried to think you could fantasize about anything and that's fine – and I still do think that, but I just don't want post like that coming through my door! (Saunders, 1995)

The director asked me and the actors about the issue of rape in the play. Pip [Donaghy] was particularly anxious about this. He was saying to me, 'Do you think that all men are rapists'? I said, 'Well no. I wouldn't be sitting in a room with you if I thought you were a rapist . . . I just wouldn't be.' Clearly all men have the equipment to be rapists, but then I have the equipment to kill someone, but does that make me a potential killer? The whole thing becomes complicated for me in *Blasted* because of the Soldier, who clearly goes around raping men where he can – part of killing someone is raping them (Saunders, 1995).

Below, Kane talks about the second sexual assault Ian carries out on Cate while she is unconscious. The stage directions read, 'He puts the gun to her head, lies between her legs, and simulates sex. As he comes **Cate** *sits bolt upright with a shout' (27).* I find that the most disturbing scene, and again it's to do with image: that thing of putting a gun to her head. It was interesting working through that in rehearsal with Pip [Donaghy]. He said, 'I'm having real problems with this scene, where I get on top of Cate, put a gun to her head and simulate sex. What am I thinking?' And when I prompted him Pip responded, 'Well, I'm imagining what it would be like to fuck someone who's dead.' And he just couldn't do what was in the script, which was quite literally an instruction to get on top of her and do it! And in the end I said, 'It's so much simpler than that. It's not about the rationale of putting a gun to a head. The answer is that it simply turns him on. It's a complete stimuli: he doesn't understand it – he just does it. It gives him an erection and so he brings himself off; and he has no understanding of it whatsoever, which is probably how a lot of pornography and fantasy work.' You don't hang around and think, 'Oh, this is to do with when my father spanked me as a child.' You just think, 'Whip me!' And it's hard for actors because they always want to know exactly what they're doing; but I think a lot of the time, particularly with Ian – well, actually with all of the characters – all they need to know is they don't know why they do it (Saunders, 1995).

I was working with some actors on a workshop about *Blasted*. Someone said, 'There's nothing unusual about the fact there were rape camps in Bosnia. That's what war is about.' Although it seems the Vietnamese troops in the Vietnam War didn't rape – they just didn't. When western women were captured by the Viet Cong, and they were finally rescued, people said, 'Oh God, what happened? Were you raped?' It was almost said gleefully for stories – and there just weren't any. There were also a large proportion of women conscripts in the Chinese army and there weren't any reported stories of rape either. Isolated incidents maybe, but it really wasn't used systematically as a war weapon. Certainly, it's happening in Yugoslavia – it's being used systematically to degrade Muslim women. So I tend to think there's got to be something cultural about that.[24]

I don't know why we want to believe that it's necessary for rape and violence to exist. But there does seem to be a desire to believe that it's natural. If I seriously thought that people were naturally violent I don't think I could carry on because what are you left with? You're left with nothing to do but for women to become separatist, and that's going to lead to disillusionment. I think most of my best friends are men: how could I possibly align that with believing they could rape someone? (Saunders, 1995).

Ian's rape in Blasted

It's interesting the way the scene was perceived. I was reading all these reviews and thinking, 'But that's not what I wrote at all'! What was being described was that a soldier comes in and randomly rapes Ian. And what they kept ignoring was the fact that the Soldier does it with a gun to his head, which Ian has done to Cate earlier – and he's crying his eyes out as he does it. I think both these things have changed that theatrical image completely (Saunders, 1995).

Productions

Below, Kane was asked about a production in Brussels directed by Yves Bombay which was informed by the serial killer Marc Dutroux. Between 1995 and 1996, Dutroux kidnapped and raped six girls between the ages of eight and nineteen. Four were killed. He was also convicted of having killed a suspected former accomplice. A number of shortcomings in the investigation culminated in a mass protest known as The White March in 1996, where an estimated 300,000 Belgians descended on the capital.

I do not think that the production in Brussels had very much to do with what I've written. It's not to say that I didn't like it, on the contrary. It's not one of those productions that I would want as a first production of one of my plays. It couldn't help me as a writer to develop. But coming from another country I found it interesting.

The play was produced at the time of the Dutroux affair. When I was in Brussels at the time, bodies were uncovered; there was an enormous amount of guilt. Whenever I met someone he was always crying, 'I am ashamed to be Belgian,' which I found quite extraordinary. I can't imagine someone saying I am ashamed of being British. *Blasted* became almost completely about a baby which dies. At the point when the baby was being buried, people in the audience were crying. I certainly felt that it was not because of the play but because of what was going on outside the theatre. The production took the play and reinterpreted it in terms of what was happening in that city. That's fine. If the situation was happening in London with a first production of a play I would be extremely unhappy, and I would probably withdraw the play (Thielemans, 1999).

In contrast Kane had little positive to say about a 1996 production of Blasted *in Hamburg, Germany.*

I went to Hamburg to see *Blasted*, and this man walked onto the stage and I thought, 'Who's that?' This guy in a really trendy leather jacket, greased back hair and wraparound sunglasses. And I thought, 'Who the fuck is that person supposed to be – this thirty year old?' And then I thought, 'Oh my God, that's supposed to be Ian and that's supposed to be a forty five year old guy!' But I thought, 'I know this character, where have I seen this character?' And then I thought, 'It's Tarantino.' And my heart just broke. I could hear this cracking in my chest.

The second scene in that production, where Cate's been raped during the night, the lights came up and she's lying there on the bed completely naked, legs apart, covered in blood and mouthing off at Ian. I just wanted to die. I said to the director, 'You know she's been raped in the night? Do you think it's either believable, interesting, feasible or theatrically valid that she's lying there completely naked in front of the man who's raped her? Do you not think she might cover herself up for example?' And that's not to do with my feelings about nudity on stage. I've been naked myself on stage [playing the role of Grace for the three final performances of *Cleansed* at the Royal Court in 1998], and I have no problem with it. It's simply about what is the truth of any given moment (Rebellato, 1998).

In Germany [*Blasted*] was received very well. But I hated the first German production in Hamburg. It completely glamorized the violence. I think the director thought it was a stage version of Tarantino. It's not. Tarantino's films certainly aren't about hope and love. Actually, they're not about violence; they're about the representation of violence. Films about film. They're

essentially self-referential. If directors took the play and transferred it to their own culture, I wouldn't mind, but that isn't
what happens. They tend to distort the play out of all recognition until it's about something totally different. It's quite
depressing to sit through so these days I go to fewer and fewer
productions abroad (Sierz, 18 January 1999).

Phaedra's Love

The Writing of the Play
It was commissioned by the Gate Theatre. They asked me to
rewrite a classic and my original choice was Woyzeck; but they
were actually planning to do a season of all of Büchner's plays,
so Woyzeck was out. Then I said I'll do Brecht's Baal because
it's loosely based on Woyzeck. But the Gate thought of all the
possible problems with the Brecht estate and we did not really
want to get into that. So in the end it was the Gate which suggested something Greek or Roman, but I've always hated those
plays. Everything happens off-stage, and what's the point? But
I decided to read one of them and see what I'd get. I chose
Seneca because Caryl Churchill had done a version of one of
his plays which I liked very much.[25] I read Phaedra, and surprisingly enough it interested me. It depicts a sexually corrupt
royal family so it's completely contemporary. This was long
before Diana [Princess of Wales] died. But there is all that stuff
in the last scene of Phaedra's Love about the most popular person in the royal family dying and so on. Now would be a really good time for a production here.

I read Euripides after I'd written Phaedra's Love. And I've
never read Racine so far. Also, I only read Seneca once. I didn't
want to get too much into it – I certainly didn't want to write a
play that you couldn't understand unless you knew the original. I wanted it to stand completely on its own.

The other interesting thing about Phaedra was that I thought
Hippolytus was so unattractive for someone supposed to be so
pure and puritanical, and I thought the way to make him

attractive is to make him unattractive but with the Puritanism inverted, because I wanted to write about an attitude to life, not a lifestyle. So I made him pursue honesty rather than sexual purity which I hadn't cared for anyway. Plus I thought you *can* subvert that convention of everything happening off-stage and have it on-stage and see how that works.

And besides, before I'd even asked the Gate about doing *Baal* I'd already done some work on my version of it, so I had these scenes with Baal and various people. And when I looked at them again I actually thought this is the same character, so I can just use this material for *Phaedra's Love*. The scene with Hippolytus and the Priest was originally written for *Baal* (Tabert, 1998).

On directing *Phaedra's Love*

The thing that I felt quite strongly about was that in lots of productions of *Blasted* sometimes I was looking at the stage and I wasn't seeing exactly the images I had written. And so I thought that if I direct *Phaedra's Love* myself there's no one to blame. If the image doesn't happen it's completely my own fault, and I find out how difficult it is. And it turned out to be a lot easier than you would think it is. I mean, you write something like, 'His bowels are torn out', and that seemed an incredibly difficult thing to do. But actually, audiences are really willing to believe something is happening if you give them the slightest suggestion that it is (Tabert, 1998).

Poetics, Greek Tragedy and Staging

I wanted to keep the classical concerns of Greek theatre – love, hate, death, revenge, suicide – but use a completely contemporary urban poetry. I see the writing as poetic. Just not verse (Benedict, 1996).

On the convention of Greek tragedy representing violence offstage

I mean, if you're not going to see what happens, why not stay at home? Why pay ten pounds to not see it? The reported deaths in Seneca are incredibly strongly written, conjuring the image really well, but personally I'd rather have an image right in front of me (Benedict, 1996).

The 1996 Gate production which Kane directed had the playing space surrounded by the audience. Actors were planted amongst the audience, who emerged during the final scene as the mob.

It meant that for any given audience member, the play could be at one moment intimate and personal, at the next epic and public. They may see one scene from one end of the theatre and find themselves sitting in the middle of a conversation for the next. And since it is a play that becomes more and more public, that's an entirely appropriate experience to have (Langridge and Stephenson, 1997).

Hippolytus

This supposedly beautiful young boy [in Seneca's version] is, to my mind, totally unattractive and other than the influence of the gods I couldn't see why Phaedra would fall in love with him. I wanted that same drive towards destruction at the end but I didn't want the passion imposed by the external force of the gods. I wanted to give it to the characters, to make it a human tragedy, so I turned him into something quite different (Benedict, 1996).

Hard to believe I know, but I was a fervent, born-again, charismatic, spirit-filled Christian . . . In a sense it's what *Phaedra's Love* is about. Like Hippolytus, I committed the unforgivable sin, which is knowing that God is real and consciously deciding to reject Him. I believed in God but not the lifestyle that Christianity demanded. I knew a lot of Christians who I thought were fundamentally bad people and a lot of non-Christians who I thought were utterly beautiful, and I couldn't understand that; so I made a conscious decision to reject God and gradually my belief subsided. According to the Bible I am now utterly damned. The point in *Phaedra's Love* is that if you're not sure God exists you can cover your arse, living your life carefully just in case, as the Priest does, or you can live your life as you want to live it. If there is a God who can't accept the honesty of that then, well, tough (Benedict, 1996).

[Hippolytus is compelled to tell the truth] and he lies as well. He lies because he confirms the rape, but at the same time he's actually telling the truth. Because it's the only way she [Phaedra] can express what he did to her and so it becomes true. But the pursuance of honesty was something that kept coming back to me when I was writing *Phaedra's Love*. The play is a comedy, but I was deeply depressed when I wrote it. And someone said to me – which ended up in the play – because I was going on and on about how important it is to tell the truth, and how depressing life is because nobody really does; and you can't have honest relationships. And he said, 'That's because you've got your values wrong. You take honesty as an absolute – and it isn't. Life is an absolute. And without that, you accept that there is dishonesty. And if you can accept that you'd be fine.' And I thought, if I can accept that if not being completely honest doesn't matter, then I'd feel much better. But somehow I couldn't, and so Hippolytus can't. And that's what kills him in the end (Tabert, 1998).

For me puritanism isn't about lifestyle, but an attitude. Instead of pursuing what is traditionally seen as pure, my Hippolytus pursues honesty, both physically and morally – even when that means he has to destroy himself and everyone else. The purity of his self-hatred makes him much more attractive as a character than the virginal original (Langridge and Stephenson, 1997).

For me Hippolytus was always sympathetic because he's always completely and utterly direct with everyone no matter what the outcome is going to be for him or for others. You can never misunderstand anything that he's saying. And I suppose that's one of the things I personally strive for – to be completely and utterly understood. Hippolytus for me is an ideal. If I was like him I'd be quite pleased with myself. He's a complete shit, but he's also very funny, and for me that's always redeeming. I think there are people who can treat you really badly, but if they do it with a sense of humour, then you can forgive them. Whether or not you should is somehow beside the point.

There's a politician here, Alan Clark, the most appallingly right-wing unpleasant person; and he fucks everyone he can. He's written his diaries now, about his affairs.[26] His behaviour is utterly revolting, but he's so funny that his diaries are utterly compelling. And somehow you forgive him. You think, well at least he's not pretending to be something he's not. He's completely open about the fact that he's sexually corrupt. He does what he wants to do. He doesn't pretend to have desires he doesn't have; he's honest about what he wants. And for some reason I admired him for that. So I love Hippolytus. But then I love Ian as well (Tabert, 1998).

The question of his dominance in the play
I suppose I did set out to write a play about depression because of my state of being at that time. And so inevitably it did become more about Hippolytus – except that it was also about that split in my own personality: of the fact that I'm simultaneously Hippolytus and Phaedra; and both those things are completely possible – that lethal cynicism coupled with obsessional love for someone who is completely unlovable. So everytime I wrote a scene I was writing myself into rather opposite states, and what it's like when these two people come together. The act of writing the play was to try to connect two extremes in my own head – which in the end wasn't only a depressing experience, but also very liberating (Tabert, 1998).

His death . . .
The thing with Hippolytus is that in his moment of death everything suddenly connects and he has one moment of complete sanity and humanity. But in order to get there he has to die. Actually, that's a bit like the Soldier in *Blasted*. There, the only way he can ever learn what his girlfriend had to go through is when he's pulling the trigger – but, of course, the next moment is the moment of his death.

I guess on a different level this is also why people slash their skin. I just met someone who has taken God knows how many overdoses and has attempted suicide in almost every imaginable way. She has a huge scar around here [points to her throat], and scars around here [points to her wrists]. But actually, she's more connected with herself than most people I know. I think in that moment when she slashes herself, when she takes an overdose, suddenly she's connected and then wants to live. And so she takes herself to hospital. Her life is an ongoing stream of suicide attempts which she then revokes. And yes, there's something really awful about that, but I can understand it very well. It makes sense to me (Tabert, 1998).

On the Character of Phaedra
Kane was asked why in Phaedra's Love *her female characters were underdeveloped in relationship to Hippolytus.*
I'd dispute the assertion that the women are underdeveloped. And I'm sure the actresses who played them would too. Phaedra is the first person to become active in the play – her accusation and suicide liberates Hippolytus and sets off the most extraordinary chain of events leading to the collapse of the monarchy (Langridge and Stephenson, 1997).

Humour in the Play
It's probably a life saving humour. When I was first thinking about writing that play I read an article in a newspaper written by a man who'd been suffering from clinical depression for three years. And he said the only thing that he'd had to

72

hang onto was this really morbid sense of humour. It was the only thing that made him bearable to be with. And that kept him rooted. I suppose that was the thing with *Phaedra's Love*. I think when you are depressed, oddly, your sense of humour is the last thing to go; when that goes then you completely lose it. And actually, Hippolytus never loses it. I don't think he's taking the piss in the last line ['If there could have been more moments like this,' 103] . . . he's aware of the paradox (Tabert, 1998).

Language in the Play
There was also something about the inadequacy of language to express emotion that interested me. In *Phaedra's Love*, what Hippolytus does to Phaedra is not rape – but the English language doesn't contain the words to describe the emotional decimation he inflicts. 'Rape' is the best word Phaedra can find for it, the most violent and potent, so that's the word she uses (Langridge and Stephenson, 1997).

The Theme of Monarchy
In *Phaedra's Love*, I tried to explore the basis of the monarchy and its relationship to the press who wanted to attack them. For me though, it speaks of depression, like there is a very evident relationship between the monarchy and depression. It's a work about a man who feels useless, and who in fact is – and is a prince (Giammarco, 1997).

Cleansed

The Writing of *Cleansed*
When people read the script, they latch on to the violent things. And yes, for me there's an enormous amount of despair in the play because I felt an enormous amount of despair when I was writing it. I started writing it before *Blasted* was produced and it's taken three-and-a-half years – I had to keep taking breaks because the material was so difficult. But there are a lot of very

beautiful things in the play too, so I'm calling it a love story even though that's not as newsworthy as saying it's about someone getting their balls chopped off (Stratton, 1998).

I was having a particular sort of fit about all of this naturalistic rubbish which was being produced; and I decided I wanted to write a play that could never be turned into a film, or shot for television, or turned into a novel. The only thing that could ever be done with it was that it could be staged. Believe it or not, that play was *Cleansed* (Rebellato, 1998).

The Theme of Love in the Play

If you want to write about extreme love, you can only write about it in an extreme way. Otherwise, it doesn't mean anything. So I suppose both *Blasted* and *Cleansed* are about distressing things which we'd like to think we would survive. If people can still love after that, then love is the most powerful thing (Armitstead, 1998).

When I was working on *Cleansed*, I was in a very extreme state. I was going through the most appalling depression, and it was about that; but then on the other hand I was so completely utterly and madly in love that those two things didn't seem to be any contradiction at all – these days it does. Sometimes when I read *Cleansed*, it's like it's by another writer. I, as I am now, could not write it. But it was never about the violence; it was about how much these people love. I think *Cleansed*, more than any of my other plays, uses violence as a metaphor (Tabert, 1998).

Below, Kane talks of how Roland Barthes' A Lover's Discourse *(1977) influenced the writing of* Cleansed. *Divided up into eighty fragments or 'figures', the book outlines in each case a particular type of lover's behaviour. Content includes personal incidents as well as references taken from literature, philosophy, proverbs, religion and music. For the most part it is written in the first person of a lover who experiences the state almost exclusively in terms of anxiety, loss and expectation. Another key idea taken from* A Lover's Discourse *that finds its way into* Cleansed *is the interrogation of the phrase 'I love you'. For Barthes, it loses meaning after its first utterance and he describes it as a 'socially irresponsible word' (p.148). Similarly, in* Cleansed, *Rod mocks Carl's expression of love by observing, 'You love me so much why can't you remember my name' (110). In an exchange of rings, Rod defines the meaning by which he understands the phrase: 'I love you now. I'm with you now. I'll do my best, moment by moment, not to betray you. Now. That's it. No more. Don't make me lie to you' (111).*

However, the influence of A Lover's Discourse *is most keenly felt in Kane's last play* 4.48 Psychosis. *Barthes saw the necessity of his book coming from the essentially solitary condition of the lover who doubts that their passion is ever fully reciprocated, or even recognised by the beloved. Like* 4.48 Psychosis *and its reference to 'the broken hermaphrodite' (205),* A Lover's Discourse *uses the same imagery to describe the unrealised state of reciprocal bliss, and both works subsequently describe the painful attempts to achieve this state of fulfilment.*[27]

Rick Rylance described A Lover's Discourse *as both 'a book of retrieval' and 'a book of the self'*[28] *– and both terms are also accurate descriptions of* 4.48 Psychosis' *themes and terms of reference. Just as Theseus in Shakespeare's* A Midsummer Night's Dream *equates 'The lunatic, the lover, and the poet' (5:1, 7) as one entity, so too do Barthes and Kane, although both observed that society all too often fails to differentiate between the figure of the suffering lover and the madman. In* 4.48 Psychosis *the lover reveals their own pathology: 'Diagnosis: Pathological grief' (223).* A Lover's Discourse *and* 4.48 Psychosis *are also essentially performative. Rylance argued that Barthes' work could equally have been renamed 'A Lover's Tragedy', and argued that the polarities of ecstasy and* *despair which define the lover's condition create 'a kind of theatre which defined the roles of extremes', and 'a theatre of the self'.*[29] *This bringing together of 'tragedy' and 'theatre of self' also illustrates the concerns of 4.48 Psychosis, whereby similar extremes are experienced by the lover who is 'dying for one who doesn't know' (243) and the figure of the beloved who always eludes definition.*

Cleansed is mainly written as a reflection of my life without it being autobiographical. There's a point in *A Lover's Discourse* by Roland Barthes when he says the situation of a rejected lover is not unlike a situation of a prisoner in Dachau.[30] And when I read it I was just appalled and thought how can he possibly suggest the pain of love is as bad as that; but then the more I thought about it actually I do know what he's saying. It's about a loss of self. And when you lose yourself where do you go? There's nowhere to go: it's actually a kind of madness. And thinking about that I made the connection with *Cleansed*. If you put people in a situation in which they lose themselves then you can make that connection between the two as long as you don't start writing things like 'Auschwitz 1944' – which would be reductive anyway (Tabert, 1998).

When you lose the object of love, you have none of the normal resources to fall back on. It can completely destroy you. And very obviously, concentration camps are about dehumanizing people before they are killed. I wanted to raise some questions about these two extreme and apparently different situations (Stratton, 1998).

The Character of Robin

Robin is based on a young black man who was on Robben Island with Nelson Mandela. He was eighteen years old. He was put on Robben Island and told he was going to be there for forty-five years. It didn't mean anything to him – he was illiterate. Nelson Mandela and some of the other prisoners taught him to read and write. He learnt to count, realised what forty-five years was and hung himself. I really don't invent very much (Rebellato, 1998).[31]

The Meaning Behind the Ritual Dismemberment of Carl

The effect we get is that we understand that someone's feet have been cut off. How you do that is a completely different thing and how you make that into a coherent production is another. But for me it's not about someone writing down how much he loves someone, so he gets his hands chopped off. It's not about the actual chop, it's about the person no longer being able to express love with his hands, and what does that mean? I think the less naturalistically you show these things, the more likely people are to be thinking, what does this mean? (Rebellato, 1998).

On Playing the Role of Grace

For its three final performances at the Royal Court in 1998, Kane played the role of Grace after the original actress Suzan Sylvester was unable to perform through injury.

There were rumours circulating that I pushed an actress down some stairs – it's not true! Her dog was trying to have sex with another dog in a park and she was pulling it off and slipped a disc. So we sat there for two days going, 'What are we going to do, could it be pushed back in place'? But the problem was that she had to be flown halfway up a wall, and do all sorts of extraordinary things, which is just not possible to do with a slipped disc. So we were going to close, at which point I got very depressed and thought I can't quite bear for the play to end in this way. Then in a moment of rashness I said, 'Well look, I know the lines, I can do it', and the next thing I knew I was being flown half-way up a wall!

I learnt how difficult acting is, and how easy acting is. Everyone makes it so very complicated, and it's really not. In fact, acting is an extremely simple thing. It's the simplicity that makes it difficult. I can't talk about all acting, but what *Cleansed* asked for was extreme simplicity, and that's an extremely difficult thing to do when you're standing in front of four hundred people with no clothes on. Your instinct is to run away, but actually it's a very simple thing. What do I want? How do I feel? And how do I enable myself to feel that?

It was interesting being the only person in the world who has been in and seen a production of *Cleansed*. It's extraordinary how different it is. It was a very different journey through the play, but one which I liked; it suddenly became extremely clear to me – they [the characters in *Cleansed*] are all just in love. It's actually very sixties and hippie. They are all emanating great love and need. The obstacles in the way are extremely unpleasant, but that's not what the play is about. Because what drives people is need, not the obstacle (Rebellato, 1998).

Crave

Origins
I walked into Vicky [Featherstone's] office one day and found she was not there. But I saw a copy of Fassbinder's *Preparadise Sorry Now*, which I started to read.[32] While reading it I suddenly had the idea of *Crave*.

In the case of *Crave*, I had a twenty-minute version after three days of writing. We did a reading at lunchtime with four different actors. Vicky had orchestrated the rhythm and by listening to it, I realised how much further I could go in terms of musicality. The 'Yes, no, yes, no' (163) sections suddenly came to my mind by listening to the rhythm and I thought, 'How extreme can I be with this'? I wouldn't have known that just by writing it at my desk (Thielemans, 1999).

The First British Performances of *Crave*
Vicky Featherstone, the director of *Crave*, has done everything in her power to make it a performance in the true sense of the word. And for me, watching the actors perform is a little like watching [Manchester] United – when they fly, they take off together, and when they don't, the collapse is truly ensemble.

We also had a nasty injury scare. During the second preview, Paul Hickey [who played B] had to stop the performance due to sudden paralysis on one side of his face. The entire company was aghast, fearing he'd had a stroke. The doctor assured us it was merely hyperventilation (read 'overacting') caused by the ludicrous demands set by my text and Vicky's insistence on performance. But it's only by making such demands that there's a chance of accurate expression of ideas and emotion, and direct intellectual, emotional and physical contact with the needs of the audience (Kane, 'Drama with Balls', 1998).

Characterisation

To me A was always an older man, M was always an older woman, B was always a younger man, and C was a woman. I decided not to specify. I thought there were things the characters said that made it very clear. For example it would be very odd if a man said, 'When I wake I think my period must have started' (156). It would also be very strange if a man kept talking about how much he wanted a baby. But on the other hand, yes, it could be done. I'm sure I'll see a production in Germany where it's done!

A, B, C and M do have specific meanings which I am prepared to tell you. A is many things: the author and abuser, because they're the same thing; Aleister as in Aleister Crowley, who wrote some interesting books that you might like to read, and the Anti-Christ.[33] My brother came up with arse-hole, which I thought was good. There was also the actor who I originally wrote it for, who was called Andrew, so that was how A came to life.[34] M was simply mother, B was boy and C was child. But I didn't want to write these things down, because then I thought they'll get fixed in those things forever and they'll never change (Rebellato, 1998).

On Its Lack of Optimism

I think *Crave* – where there is no physical hope whatsoever, it's a very silent play – is the most despairing of the things

I've written so far. At some point somebody says, 'Something has lifted,' (196) and from that moment on it becomes apparently more and more hopeful: but actually all the characters have given up. It's the first one of my plays in which people go, 'Fuck this, I'm out of here' . . . *Crave* was written during the process of ceasing to have faith in love. And it's odd that at that stage I seemed to write something that was less violent and maybe ultimately less depressing for other people (Tabert, 1998).

The way the play was received surprised me, as it was said to be extremely positive [in tone]. My previous work was called very despairing, but there was a ray of hope, some people felt. But for me this play is about despair and suicide. It was written at a time when I felt quite despairing, that is probably the reason why (Thielemans, 1999).

Ascribing Meaning in the Play

I was trying to do something different with *Crave* which was in a way about not really releasing control, but about opening up options. In some ways for me, *Crave* is very specific. It has very fixed and specific meanings in my mind, which no one else can possibly know, unless I told them. For example, who here knows what 199714424 means (188)? None of you knows. I'm the only person that knows – besides the actors – and I've no intention of telling anyone what it means. So I can't possibly expect to ever see the same production twice (Rebellato, 1998).

4.48 Psychosis

I've just started to work on a new play: [*laughs*] awful isn't it – yet another play which is about the split between one's consciousness and one's physical being. For me that's what madness is about. And the only way back to any kind of sanity is to connect physically with who you are emotionally, spiritually and mentally.

Now my entire work is moving more and more towards poetry. It's most obvious in *Crave*. It was strange. When I finished *Crave*, I thought that I didn't know where to go. But when I started this one [*4.48 Psychosis*] just a few weeks ago, I suddenly realised that it goes further. At the moment it doesn't even have characters – there is only language and images. But all the images are within language rather than visualised. I don't even know how many people there are (Tabert, 1998).

I'm writing a play called *4.48 Psychosis*. It's got similarities with *Crave*, but it's different. It's about a psychotic breakdown, and what happens to the person's mind when the barriers which distinguish between reality and the forms of imagination completely disappear – so that you no longer know the difference between your waking life and your dream life. It's very interesting in psychosis that you no longer know where you stop and the world starts. So for example, if I was psychotic I would literally not know the difference between myself and this table. They would all somehow be part of a continuum, and various boundaries begin to collapse. Formally, I'm beginning to collapse a few boundaries as well and to carry on with making the form and content one. That's proving extremely difficult, and I'm not going to tell any of you how I'm doing it, because if any of you get there first I shall be furious! Whatever I began with *Crave* it's going a step further, and for me there's a very clear line from *Blasted* to *Phaedra's Love*, to *Cleansed*, to *Crave* – and this one is going on through. Where it goes after that I'm not sure (Rebellato, 1998).

On Theatre and Television Drama

The Need for Theatre
I am convinced that the theatre is part of the most fundamental of human needs. I believe that if a city is destroyed by a bomb, the people first of all look for food and shelter, and having provided these necessities they start to tell their stories.[35]

For me the function of the theatre is to allow experimentation through art in a way that we are not able to experiment effectively in real life. If we experiment in the theatre, such as an act of extreme violence, then maybe we can repulse it as such, to prevent the act of extreme violence out on the street. I believe that people can change and that it is possible for us as a species to change our future. It's for this that I write what I write (Giammarco, 1997).

If theatre can change lives, then by implication it can change society, since we're all part of it. I also think it's important to remember that theatre is not an external force acting on society, it's part of it, a reflection of the way people within that society view the world. Slasher movies don't create a violent society (though they may well perpetuate it); they're a product of that society. Films, books, theatre, they all represent something which already exists, even if only in someone's head, and through the representation they can change or reinforce what they describe (Langridge and Stephenson, 1997).

I think the obsession with content that the critics have means that any play which contains scenes of violence will be seen as a violent play rather than a play about violence, because they don't know how to talk about it – and that's exacerbated by the fact that theatre is a live art. You can go along to see the film *Natural Born Killers*, eat popcorn, snog in the back row, walk out if you don't like it and it makes absolutely no difference to the images that are being projected onto the screen. Whereas if you indulge in that activity in the theatre you disrupt the performance, and that's a reciprocal relationship between the performers and the audience. I think if we want a theatre – and I do – which is able to deal with the full range of human emotion, then it must be able to represent the full range of human experience – no matter how violent and supposedly degrading that is (*Start the Week*, 1995).

We realised halfway through the shoot [of *Skin*] that it was too long and so we had to be brutal about cutting, which I really enjoyed . . . trying to hang on to the poetry of the writing but at the same time being really functional. I'm not keen on over indulgence. I know nobody would agree with me on that (Benedict, 1996).

In a piece of journalism, Kane draws an analogy between her love of both football and theatre.

Bollocks to [The] Edinburgh [Festival] – I'm off to Old Trafford. First day of the season and the sun is shining on the Theatre of Dreams. But the first 85 minutes are a nightmare. United are 2–0 down to Leicester with five minutes to go. The crowd start to leave. [Teddy] Sheringham scores, but with only a minute left I'm on the verge of saying, 'Bollocks to football – I'm off to the festival'. Then a miracle occurs. In the last minute we're awarded a free kick 30 yards out. David Beckham steps up and curls it into the back of the net. A stiff two fingers to everyone in the country who hates him for being rich, talented and shagging that bird. The talents of myself and writer-director Vincent O'Connell are very nearly lost to the nation as we disappear through the roof of the North Stand.

I frequently walk out of the theatre early without fear of missing anything. But however bad I've felt, I've never left a football match early, because you never know when a miracle might occur.

The sexual connotations of 'performance' are not coincidental. Liverpool's Paul Ince publicly admits that he finds tackling more enjoyable than sex. Performance is visceral. It puts you in direct physical contact with thought and feeling. When I write about United's performance, I can't help but write in the present tense.

I saw the Jesus and Mary Chain[36] at the foot of Edinburgh Castle a few nights back, and found myself longing for a theatre that could speak so directly to an audience's experience. It rarely happens.

But it happened at *The Ladyboys of Bangkok*,[37] with the sheer joy of seeing a Thai transsexual lip-synching to *I Am What I Am*. And it happened when I stumbled upon the Zimbabwean Nasa Theatre dancing and drumming to an exuberant crowd on the Lothian Road.[38]

It also happened at the Mona Hatoum exhibition at the Scottish National Gallery of Modern Art. In a tiny cylindrical room I watched a projection of a surgical camera disappearing into every orifice of the artist. True, few people could stay in the room as long as me, but I found that the voyage up Mona Hatoum's arse put me in powerful and direct contact with my feelings about my own mortality.[39] I can't ask for much more (Kane, 'Drama with Balls', 1998).

I hate the idea of theatre just being an evening pastime. It should be emotionally and intellectually demanding. I love football. The level of analysis that you listen to on the terraces is astonishing. If people did that in the theatre . . . but they don't. They expect to sit back and not participate. If there's a place for musicals, opera or whatever, then there should be a place for good new writing, irrespective of box office. What do we want our culture to be remembered for in a hundred years time: *Neighbours*? (Nightingale, 1995).

The critic John Peter made the following comment on seeing Blasted: *'Kane's vision is born of unleavened, almost puritanical moral outrage; and outrage, like violence, needs careful handling in the theatre . . . how much despair can you show, before an audience is overdosed'?*[40] *Here, Kane responds to this criticism.* Most people experience a lot more despair and brutality than John Peter would like to believe. There's only the same danger of overdose in the theatre as there is in life. The choice is either to represent it, or not represent it. I've chosen to represent it because sometimes we have to descend into hell imaginatively in order to avoid going there in reality. If we can experience something through art, then we might be able to change our future, because experience engraves lessons on our heart through suffering, whereas speculation leaves us untouched. And anyone – politician, journalist, artist – who attempts to give people that imaginative experience, faces derisive screams that it's too much from all sections of the artistic and social spectrum. It's crucial to chronicle and commit to memory events never experienced – in order to avoid them happening. I'd rather risk overdose in the theatre than life. And I'd rather risk defensive screams than passively become part of a civilization that has committed suicide (Langridge and Stephenson, 1997).

On Film/Television Drama

I would never work in television, and they wouldn't let me.[41] There is too much censorship. As you cannot say what you want to say, I will not do it. Before Dennis Potter died, I already decided not to write for television.[42] Film is another matter. I've written one ten minute film [Skin], which was made for television, but they would not show it until after midnight – that says it all.[43] My decision though is not only due to the censorship. I decided on theatre because it's a live art. This direct communication with an audience I really like. As a writer, I like the fact that no two performances will ever be the same (Thielemans, 1999).

But [the] Edinburgh [Festival] in August isn't only about theatre. Frequently, the theatre-makers don't know there's a film festival on, the filmmakers don't know there's a television festival and the television-makers don't even know they're in Scotland. This year's highlight for me looks to be the Alan Clarke retrospective.[44]

Though he directed some of the greatest television films ever made, the industry Clarke worked in couldn't appreciate him until he was dead. And perhaps that is the key to the nostalgia surrounding the fringe (Kane, 'The Only Thing I Remember Is', 1998).

On Theatre Critics

After *Blasted*, I moved to New York for six months and then I decided to move back. Suddenly London had become reinstated as my home. I'd become absolutely sick of London. The reason I had at the time was different from what I think the reason was now. The reason I had at the time was personal. The reason I think now was that I was a lot more hurt by what happened to *Blasted*. It wasn't important, and I didn't take it seriously, but somewhere I don't think I acknowledged that I was very angry. I think I realised it at the very first press night of *Phaedra's Love*. A couple of particularly obnoxious critics came in and I looked at them and just felt so enraged. I didn't realise that I cared about them at all. Getting a bad review doesn't matter, but when *Skin* was on television here [the UK], when I was in New York, my parents were getting 'phone calls from the *Guardian* and the *Independent* and it made me really angry. They said the film was racist. I don't care about that, but it does matter when they start 'phoning my family. But then my Dad's been doing that his entire life – he's a tabloid journalist. He doesn't complain about it, but it bothers me (Christopher, 1997).

You see it's almost an oxymoron for me – good theatre critic, military intelligence, Christian Scientist, free love . . . I think George Bernard Shaw, possibly one of the best ever theatre critics was of course a writer. I think the best critics are people who are writers, whether or not they write for a living. I think that what generally happens with theatre critics is that they see their job – whether they acknowledge this consciously or not – is to destroy people, and they do their utmost to do it, they really do. But I think if they also have another – I hate the word career, but if they have another line of interest in art, then they're far less likely to do that.

I'd quite like to review plays. In fact I got asked to review Harold Pinter's *Ashes to Ashes* in the *Observer*, and I was really keen to do it.[45] They 'phoned up and said, 'If you don't like it that would be great'. I thought, this was a complete set-up, so I didn't want to do it. But I think playwrights reviewing other plays would be really interesting. I think that genuinely caring whether the play is good and actually wanting it to be good are prerequisites, and not the kind of joy in how vitriolic you can be (Rebellato, 1998).

On Stanislavski

I read a lot of Stanislavski. I find him interesting for an actor or a director. But you read his books and then you throw them away. If there is anything interesting in there, you have to ignore it when you work – otherwise you end up imitating someone and before you know it, you belong to a movement. God forbid! (Thielemans, 1999)

On Artaud

A lot of people said to me for a long time that I must really like Artaud, and I hadn't read any of that. Artaud was recommended to me by a lecturer at university who I hated so much that I thought, 'Well I'm not going read it if he thinks Artaud is good – he simply can't be'! So I only started reading him very recently. And the more I read it [the more] I thought this is a definition of sanity: this man is completely and utterly sane and I understand everything he's saying. And I was amazed how it connects completely with my work. Also, his writings about theatre are stunningly good. And it's amazing to me that I'd never read it. But Artaud is the first one of that bunch of writers. I'm sure when I've got through him I'll move on to Bataille.[46] I also think depression is quite a healthy state of being because all it reflects is a completely realistic perception of what's going on. I think to a certain degree you have to deaden your ability to feel and perceive. In order to function you have to cut out at least one part of your mind; otherwise you'd be chronically sane in a society which is chronically insane.

I mean look at Artaud. That's your choice: go mad and die or function but be insane (Tabert, 1998).

On Directing

When I was asked to direct *Woyzeck* there were only four plays that I would have agreed to direct and *Woyzeck* was one of them. The others are [George Bernard Shaw's] *Man and Superman*, Brecht's *Baal* and Bond's *Lear*.

At university I directed *Top Girls*, *Low Level Panic*, *Macbeth*, *Rockaby* and *I Don't Move I Don't Scream My Voice Has Gone* [by Franca Rame.⁴⁷] I also did shows called *Dreams Screams and Silences* and *Dreams Screams Number 2*, which were a collection of short plays by Vincent O'Connell. We had ten short plays, and at the beginning of each show, someone from the audience gave Vince a title and while the show was on, he wrote a new play. And then actors read it at the end and we rehearsed it the following morning – took an old play out and put the new one in – so by the end of the run there was a completely new set of plays. We did that two years in a row at Edinburgh. I also wrote three monologues under the collective title of *Sick* [*Comic Monologue, Starved* and *What She Said*]. Two of them I performed, and I directed other people in them at Edinburgh, Bristol and London.

My approach to directing is pretty much the same as my approach to writing, which is not to start with a style – start with a style and it's fucked from the beginning. But if you go from moment to moment and go for the truth of each moment then the sum total of that is the style. And then people can call it whatever they want to call it. If you get each moment right then the whole thing will work. That way you cut out a hundred thousand options before you've even started.

I didn't want to direct *Blasted* because I was very deliberately going for each moment. At times I would stop and think, 'How do you do this'? And I had to say, 'I can't think about this – it's not my problem. I've just got to write what I want to write'. When I looked at the finished script, I thought I wouldn't know how to do this. I want someone else to find out. And the next couple of things I've written I wouldn't want to direct either – but that's also partly to do with how intense it is to write. For example, *Crave* was extremely intense to write but for a far shorter period of time.

I suppose with something that I've written, there are things about it that I don't know which I need to find out at rehearsal; but if the actors can't find anything there's always something to fall back on. I know where it comes from even if I don't always know what it means. Whereas with something that someone else has written, especially if they're dead, you don't necessarily know what the impulse is behind the moment or the scene. So there are many more times when an actor asks what's it about and I say I don't know, whereas with *Phaedra's Love*, often I would say I don't know what it's about but here's where it started (Christopher, 1997).

Dramatic Form

Blasted

All good art is subversive, either in form or content. And the best art is subversive in form *and* content. And often, the element that most outrages those who seek to impose censorship is form. Beckett, Barker, Pinter, Bond – they have all been criticised not so much for the content of their work, but because they use non-naturalistic forms that elude simplistic interpretation (Langridge and Stephenson, 1997).

Kane expands on her point about dramatic form often being responsible for censorship in a later interview with Aleks Sierz. If you're in any doubt about that, you only have to consider why Stalin censored Soviet composers.[48] Evidently, it wasn't the content of their work, it wasn't the individual notes that so disturbed him, it was the truly revolutionary forms that he found subversive to his dictatorship (Sierz, 18 January 1999).

I suspect that if *Blasted* had been a piece of social realism it wouldn't have been so harshly treated. The form and content attempted to be one – the form is the meaning. The tension in the first half of the play, this appalling social, psychological and sexual tension, is almost a premonition of the disaster to come. And when it does come, the structure fractures to allow its entry. The play collapses into one of Cate's fits. The form is a direct parallel to the truth of the war it portrays – a traditional form is suddenly and violently disrupted by the entrance of an unexpected element that drags the characters and the play into a chaotic pit without logical explanation. In terms of Aristotle's Unities, the time and action are disrupted while unity of place is retained – which caused a great deal of offence because it implied a direct link between domestic violence in Britain and civil war in the former Yugoslavia. *Blasted* raised the question: 'What does a common rape in Leeds have to do with mass rape as a war weapon in Bosnia?' And the answer appeared to be 'Quite a lot'. The unity of place suggests a paper-thin wall between the safety and civilization of peacetime Britain and the chaotic violence of civil war. A wall that can be torn down at any time, without warning.

I think critics have a problem discussing theatrical imagery. We've been reduced to this fear of the word so much. What's the point of writing a play that doesn't have an image structure? But that image structure seemed to be completely ignored in *Blasted*, and it takes away the meaning; then they just take the meaning from the words, which is why I end up being accused of being racist and the characters as racist. You have to look at the context of the image (Saunders, 1995).

The particular form of *Blasted* doesn't have a theatrical precedent as far as I know. At least I couldn't find one. I think that once a theatrical form is invented and used, it's redundant. If *Blasted* had used a conventional form, it wouldn't have worked. The shock was not about the content; it was about the arrangement of that content into an unfamiliar form which put the audience through the experience of collapse. The nature of that experience is such that it was not possible to fully locate oneself in relation to the material. The playwright more or less abandoned the audience to craft their own response to the imagery and content by denying them the safety of familiar form (Sierz, 18 January 1999).

I think in the first draft the Soldier literally began appearing at different points. It was like Ian hallucinating and I thought this is awful, like some kind of American expressionism. I think that what happens in war is that suddenly, violently, without any warning whatsoever, people's lives are completely ripped to pieces. So I literally just picked a moment in the play: I thought, 'I'll plant a bomb and blow the whole fucking thing up'! I loved the idea of it as well – you have a nice little box set in a studio theatre somewhere and you blow it up. You go to the Bush [Theatre], and you see the set and go, 'Oh no'! There's always a longing for it to blow up, so it was such a joy for me to be able to do that! (Rebellato, 1998)

Blasted was published before we went into rehearsal, and there were certain things where I thought I could take the image further.[49] For example, when Ian shits and then tries to clean it up. It's now completely clear to me that he should clean it up with newspaper. From the moment he comes into the hotel room and throws the newspapers on the bed (3), we have to follow those newspapers right the way through: they have their own story in there and that's what they're full of – shit. That's the logical conclusion. Also, the use of rain was discovered in rehearsals. This was James Macdonald's idea about having rain between scenes which gradually gets harder and harder to the point where it comes through the roof, which I think is really good.[50] It's now in my version of the script, and if there's a new edition it'll be changed (Saunders, 1995).[51]

Directors frequently think the second half of *Blasted* is a metaphor, dream, nightmare – that's the word Cate uses – and that it's somehow more abstract than the first half. In a production that works well, I think the first half should seem incredibly real and the second half even more real. Probably by the end we should be wondering if the first half was a dream (Sierz, 18 January 1999).

The baby-eating scene

A lot of people said to me when they read the scene before it was performed that they weren't sure about the baby-eating scene. I kept looking at the scene and thinking, 'Is it gratuitous? What does gratuitous mean anyway?' And does it become unbelievable? Samuel Johnson said that when Shakespeare's *King Lear* is read, the blinding of Gloucester is somehow more acceptable than experiencing a performance of the play.[52] I find the opposite. Reading *Blasted* is much harder work than watching it, because when you read it the stage directions say, '*He eats the baby*' (60). When you see the actual play Ian's clearly not eating the baby – it's absolutely fucking obvious! This is a theatrical image. So, in a way it's more demanding because it throws you back on your own imagination. But somehow, it's more realistic because you simply get the act (Saunders, 1995).

On editing

If I was going to rewrite *Blasted* again I'd look much more closely at the images of purification, and I'd cut even more words if such a thing is possible, because for me the language of theatre is image (Saunders, 1995).

Crave is at the other end of the scale, it's got more words than any of my other plays, but it's actually half the length of anything else I've written. Again, there's no waste. I don't like writing things you really don't need, and my favourite exercise is cutting – cut, cut, cut! I'm much hated at script meetings at the Royal Court. I read people's plays and inevitably I think '. . . if you just cut that line' – and it's become kind of a habit. But I think it's a good one (Rebellato, 1998).

On subtext

I was doing this workshop in Birmingham the other day and someone said to me, 'I just want to know what you think about subtext because I'm writing an essay about it'. I gave the following example that if you were from Poland I can say to you, 'Where are you from? And what would you answer?' And she said, 'Poland'. I said, 'Right, if I was writing this as a scene, what I'd have is me asking where you were from and you asking if I was racist'. That is what subtext is. It's when nobody answers the question. Everyone goes around it in some way. Everyone puts up some kind of barrier, and I don't think it's deliberate. I think it's something we do all the time. And I suppose that is what happened with *Blasted*. It started off literally with what everyone thinks and feels. The whole thing about Ian's wife Stella (18–19) – there was fucking reams of it: absolutely reams of it. But I thought it was more interesting because she becomes everyone's wife who leaves them for another woman. So, Stella becomes more universal the less detail we're given (Saunders, 1995).

Cleansed

That play can only be staged: now you may say it can't be staged, but it can't be anything else either – that's the point. It can only be done in a theatre. Of course, I knew they were impossible stage directions, but I also genuinely believe that you can do anything on stage. It's completely impossible to do *Cleansed* naturalistically, because half the audience would die from sheer grief if you did that play naturalistically. But that was kind of the point. I never asked for people to actually chop legs off, or real rats (Rebellato, 1998).

I don't know what James [Macdonald] will do about them [the rats]. I have to say, I'm glad it's not my problem. There's a Jacobean play with the stage direction, 'Her spirit rises out of her body and walks away, leaving her body behind'.[53] Anyway, Shakespeare has a bear running across the stage in *A Winter's*

Tale, and his stagecraft was perfect, so I don't know why I can't have rats (Armitstead, 1998).[54]

I think with a lot of other plays there are things from Greek drama – a messenger comes on – all of which is much easier to take and gives you time to calm down. But [in *Cleansed*] I didn't want to give anyone time to calm down. I wanted to strip everything down. I wanted it to be small. And when I say small, I mean minimal – poetic. And I didn't want to waste any words. I really hate wasted words (Rebellato, 1998).

Crave

Crave is more than what it is about. I was very deliberately looking for a different form. I wanted to find out how a poem could still be dramatic. It's deliberately an experiment with form, and language and rhythm and music.

With *Crave*, I knew what the rhythm was, but I did not know what I was going to say. There were a couple of times I used musical notation – only the rhythm without actual words. With *Crave*, the narrative strands are not chronological. I can hear people say the most bizarre things in strange situations. For me it was simply that I submerged myself in writing. It is not insignificant that I wrote it while I was living in America where no one could understand my accent at all. I was completely losing my articulacy. There was hardly a reason for speaking, as no one could understand me. So for me it's extremely important that the director constantly understands what I am trying to say and realises it in the best way possible, so that I can see where it's going out of shape and correct it.

With *Crave*, I did not see the staging. I saw the images that I had. I saw the girl in the car etcetera (157–8). I saw the images that are described. Those images I embedded in the language. But I didn't see the actors on a stage. On other occasions I saw very definite stage images (Thielemans, 1999).

Increasingly, I'm finding performance much more interesting than acting; theatre more compelling than plays. Unusually for me, I'm encouraging my friends to see my play *Crave* before reading it, because I think of it more as text for performance than as a play (Kane, 'Drama with Balls', 1998).

On contemporary British playwriting

When I left university, the first job I had was at the Bush Theatre as a Literary Assistant. I spent a lot of time reading scripts and talking with the literary managers. I hated not only almost everything that I read but definitely everything that was produced. If I wrote a report saying a play was absolutely dreadful, I could be pretty sure that it was going to be on in six months, and it was always to do with form. I'm personally very tired with seeing plays about disaffected groups of youths exploring their sexuality on a night on the beach.[55] It's really hard to characterize those plays (Rebellato, 1998).

On the relatively small audiences her work attracts

In terms of what happens to my work after I die, it's really got nothing to do with me. I'm not going to be here. I hope people write better plays, I mean that's all I can hope. But I doubt if they will. I mean rubbish has always been produced through the ages; mediocrity has always been praised. That's simply what happens. Most big plays are only really liked in retrospect – with hindsight.

When *Cleansed* was at the Royal Court, there was one point at which we were playing to very small audiences. I saw – God knows where it was on – this bit of old TV footage of some actors who were in *Serjeant Musgrave's Dance*: one of the most brilliant plays of the last hundred years.[56] And one of the actors was saying, 'You know, we don't understand it. We think it's a really good play and last night no one turned up to see it'. And you think about it now – how it's become such a classic. I think that anything to which no one turns up at some point is bound to turn out to be quite good. Anything that serves to pack out audiences, well there's probably something wrong with it (Rebellato, 1998).

On the influence her writing might have had on existing and emerging dramatists
There's been quite a negative influence. Two weeks after *Blasted* was on, I was given a script to read by the Royal Court, which was about three people in a basement roasting a body and then eating it. And I thought, 'I wonder if this person has seen *Blasted*?' There were some extraordinary similarities, including even lines. There have been a whole glut of *Blasted* copies, none of which were produced I'm pleased to say.

In terms of a positive influence, I do think there is beginning to be a move away from Naturalism. I haven't seen the new Nick Grosso play but I'm told that there's a huge leap away from Naturalism. Is that correct [*Dan Rebellato, the interviewer, replies, 'A hop'*]? A hop, a side step? Okay, but I think if that's true in terms of Nick Grosso's work, it's probably quite significant given what he's written before.[57] But I don't know, you can never anticipate these things. It's like saying, will this play still be produced in fifty years time? Will any of us be here in fifty years time? (Rebellato, 1998).

On Writing

The Role of the Dramatist
The truth is I've only ever written to escape from hell and it's never worked. But at the other end of it, when you sit there and watch something and think, well that's the most perfect expression of the hell I felt, then maybe it was worth it (Rebellato, 1998).

I do not have a responsibility as a writer. The only responsibility is towards the truth, however awful the truth might be. I do not feel a responsibility towards the audience or to other women. What I always do when I write is to think, 'How does the play affect myself.' If you are very specific in what you try to achieve, and it affects yourself, then it may affect other people too. On the other hand, if you have a target group in mind, and you think, 'I want to affect the 11 million people watching ITV on Sunday', then everything becomes bland. So for me I'm quite happy to aim at the smallest audience possible, which is myself because I am the only person who is definitely going to see this play anyway. I have directed my own work, some work by a living author and also texts by dead writers. I actually do not have the ability to be in the rehearsal room with the [dead] writer. Directing is a different skill. After all, I am a writer in the first place. Then I am a director, and in some cases, when I am under extreme pressure, I act (Thielemans, 1999).

The MA Playwriting Programme at Birmingham University

I started by being an actor. I went to [Bristol] University and studied drama. After a few productions, I decided I did not like acting very much. So I became a director. Then as a director, I needed plays and decided to write my own. I do not remember why I did it, but I decided to apply for an MA in playwriting in Birmingham. I got funding, and that was the only reason I went really, because I needed the money. I didn't actually finish the course.[58] When I was there, I wrote the first half of *Blasted* and then I moved to London. The course itself was very academic. I did not think that was very useful. I did not go to most of the lectures because I felt that they were inhibiting my writing. Living in Birmingham for a year helped me more as an artist by just making me feel miserable. I was living in a city that I simply hated. The only thing it really gave me was that I decided I wanted to write plays set in a very large industrial city, which was extremely unpleasant. That is what I did, and it became *Blasted*. In some respects [Birmingham] helped me, but at the same time you could say that is simply where I was in my life. In London, I read a fairly finished version [of *Blasted*] to the Royal Court and they said they'd pay me to finish it, or they would commission a new work. I took the commission but finished *Blasted* anyway. It was part of my Machiavellian scheme! (Thielemans, 1999)

The problem I had with the course was the same problem I had at Bristol [University] – it's an academic course and I didn't want to be an academic. Inevitably, what you're studying is what's already been discovered. As a writer, I wanted to do things that hadn't been done, to invent new modes of representation. So sitting in seminars discussing the three-act structure switched me off completely.

Also the writers I was interested in talking to – Edward Bond, Howard Barker[59] and Harold Pinter – weren't the ones who were coming in to talk to us. It was simultaneously academic and anecdotal and I can't see the usefulness of that.

I wrote the first forty-five minutes of *Blasted* [up to the entrance of the Soldier] while I was in Birmingham and it was given a workshop performance at the end of the course. It was really well directed by Pete Wynne-Wilson and I had a couple of very good student actors [Greg Hobbs and Alison Hale]. I moved to London and started working at the Bush as a Literary Assistant while I finished writing the play (Sierz, 4 January 1999).

On being asked about the process of writing
For me it is very difficult to speak about, because in all truth after I have written something the period of real writing has become an empty space. It is extremely difficult to remember it straight away. So all of my plays in general have a beginning in my mind and heart, be it six months or six years before I put it onto paper. Many of the plays contain memories or imaginings that I've had in my mind since I was a child, and also contain fragments of conversations heard on the street or in my family a long time ago. With the exception of *Cleansed*, which is the thing I absolutely found the most difficult to write and demanded an incredible length of time, the period of actual writing is relatively short. I believe that part of the reason is that I do not

wish to live with a play for a minute longer than necessary. The period of rewriting tends to be longer, but is a technical rather than an emotional experience (Giammarco, 1997).

On being asked if she makes any money
Certainly not from England, but it's the European productions that make it possible for me not to have to do a day job. But then I never have. Even before *Blasted* was produced, I refused to do anything other than write. And I was extremely poor then; whereas now I somehow keep my head above water (Tabert, 1998).

British New Writing Theatres and Companies

I think that companies such as Paines Plough, the Royal Court and the Bush are important because they do new work. These companies create theatre history. When you have your play produced for the first time as a writer, and it is not done in the way you've written it, you never see what is right; you never see where it could have gone further. Actually, when a theatre does that to you, it's harming you because you are never going to write a play that is virtually better. I had productions in the UK, in London, which have so far been committed to the text. Companies such as Paines Plough consider the author as the primary artist. I don't think that attitude is always the right thing, especially if the writer is dead. If you do a terrible production of Shakespeare it does not actually matter. You are not going to ruin his next play. But if someone messes up a first production of a play of mine, there is a good chance I won't write again. It is a huge responsibility on the part of the director.

How much . . . the Royal Court actually develops you as an artist is a different question. It makes you feel that there is a theatre that is interested in what you write. It's also difficult to say whether the Royal Court was helpful. But still, it's very nice to have a group of people who help and support you. For example, when I wrote *Crave* it's hard to say just how far Paines Plough actually helped me to write it. But the fact is that

I would never have written it if I hadn't been there . . . There have certainly been many times when I walked into the office of Paines Plough while there were authors drinking coffee. It's simply a place where you want to meet each other and support each other (Thielemans, 1999).

On Violence

Blasted

The violence in this play is completely de-glamorized. It's just presented . . . Take the glamour out of violence and it becomes utterly repulsive. Would people seriously prefer it if the violence were appealing? You'd think people would be able to tell the difference between something that's about violence and something that's violent. I don't think it's violent at all. It's quite a peaceful play (Nightingale, 1995).

The first previews of *Blasted* at the Royal Court – before I had any idea of quite how extreme the reaction was going to be – we had a couple of people walk out and it didn't surprise me. And now I think it's bound to happen. If it doesn't then it's probably because something is not working – at least something is happening; it does mean people aren't asleep. I've seen productions of *Blasted* where there was no reason to walk out because somehow they [the characters] never connected emotionally; you could completely distance yourself from what was going on. It was very easy to just sit there thinking, 'This is ridiculous, and offensive and silly and I don't care'. Whereas the production at the Royal Court was much more about emotional violence than physical violence – and that makes it a lot harder to watch it.

With *Blasted* you do know what this situation is even though it's not specifically defined; and it's a two way thing because the Soldier is the way he is because of the situation – but the situation exists because of what Ian has created in that room; of what he has done to Cate – and he does it with this deprecating self-pity which seems to me completely accurate. When people are intensely violent they manage to make the victim feel guilty. So, basically it's a completely self-perpetuating circle of emotional and physical violence. If you skip the connection between all this: if you skip the emotional reason, the play does appear to be completely broken-backed – just split into two halves which means it fails totally (Tabert, 1998).

Probably the most telling line in *Blasted* comes from the Soldier when Ian says 'Not like that', and the Soldier says, 'Not like that, they're all like that' (44). He knows he isn't like this. He hasn't always been like this – but in order to survive the war he has to live like this.

And if you look at the soldiers who survive wars, those who survive aren't the big tough ones – they're the ones who get obliterated. The ones who survive are the geeky ones who are psychopaths. Because the only way to survive chaotic violence is to be chaotically violent and completely internalise that. But on the other hand, I remember meeting a child once who was about six or seven. And I thought, 'He's going to rape someone – give him twenty years'. He was so deeply unpleasant – the sexual abuse he was hurling just horrified me. And I don't want to believe that a child was born like that, but I don't know where it comes from, unless he's being abused himself. Who knows? In a way I think maybe it doesn't matter where it comes from. What matters is dealing with it. I think Edward Bond is right in the sense that if we had a human need for violence – a kind of biological need for it we would die out as a species.[60] It's like square fish who can't swim, therefore they die out. I think we would start seeking situations in which to satisfy that need and would die out in a secular version of original sin which I can't really subscribe to. So I suppose it comes from the situation we've created for ourselves. Whose fault is that? It's a chicken and egg. In order to create a situation there must be some kind of violent intent (Saunders, 1995).

I hate the idea of drama as journalism, but when it comes to acts of violence, my imagination isn't that fucking sick. I just read the newspapers. It's not like there's something wrong with me. All you have to do is look at the world around you, and there it is. I agree with you, *Blasted* is pretty devastating, but the only reason that it's any more devastating than anything you read in the newspaper is because all of the boring bits are cut out (Rebellato, 1998).

Violence in *Phaedra's Love*
We made a decision that I would try to do the violence as realistically as possible. If it didn't work then we'd try something else, but that was a starting point to see how it went. The very first time we did the final scene with all the blood and the false bowels, by the end we were all severely traumatised; all the actors were standing there covered in blood, having just raped and slit their throats – and then one of them said, 'This is the most disgusting play I've ever been in,' and he walked out. But because of the work we'd done before, all of us knew that that point was reached because of a series of emotional journeys that had been made; so none of us felt it was unjustified – it was just completely unpleasant (Tabert, 1998).

On Violence in General
I believe, and without doubt believed during the period I was writing *Blasted*, that violence is the most urgent problem we have as a species, and the most urgent thing we need to confront. Personally, I say there is nothing better to write about. I don't like violent films, that's true, and I don't like violent scenes; and the reason I don't like violence is when I happen to see *Reservoir Dogs*, *Pulp Fiction* or other films of that type I feel like using violence. When I wrote *Blasted* I tried to discuss what it means to be violent and to suffer violence, and it's like the music that's played when you're cutting off an ear. You are in a state of extreme suffering; it's not possible you can like it for the music.[61]

I was violent for the first time when I was eight years old, and I can never forget the feeling that it produced in me. Yet, very often, when suggestions of violent acts are on the news, or I see violent films, those feelings are not completely subdued. The scale of emotions that become stimulated are completely different and often can escalate.

People have often asked me if it's really necessary to bring the things I have into a scene, and many journalists in particular have said, 'We know that these things happen, why do we need to see them?' And I believe that the answer is that we need to see the things we already know happen, but to see them presented in a different way and so will understand them better (Giammarco, 1997).

On the wireless programme Start the Week, *the topic of discussion was violence. One of the guests was the American director Oliver Stone. His film* Natural Born Killers *(1994) had recently been released in Britain and had aroused controversy over its depiction of violence. Here, Kane takes issue with Stone's assertion that the propensity for human aggression is innate.*

I don't see how it can be a natural phenomena for us in the same way as animals. I think there's a contradiction. I don't think you can draw a parallel between what you're calling natural violence – for example being ripped out of your mother's womb or hunting – and actions such as murdering people. The basic difference is that one is based on survival and the other is based on a genuinely violent emotion. And though to an extent the result of those feelings may be the same, the intention is different (*Start the Week*, 1995).

In the same discussion, geneticist Professor Steve Jones commented that genes might possibly be a factor in determining criminality. Although Jones himself was sceptical of this view and felt that societal factors were far more influential, Kane took him to task for his comment.

I fail to understand how there can be a gene for criminality at all since crime is culturally defined. One day you can go out for a peaceful protest and go to a party in the evening and that's perfectly legal. The next day the Criminal Justice Act comes into force and you're a criminal.[62] So I don't see how that can have anything to do with genetics. So I think, as I understand it, what you're saying is that there's a kind of gene for naughtiness – that one has a tendency to break those social codes, whatever those social codes may be. Now the thing is as Rosie [the journalist Rose Boycott, one of the other discussion panellists] was saying, do we abort these genetically deformed foetuses? And my feeling is if I were a woman who wanted a child and was pregnant with a child who suffered from this so called 'deformity' I'd have the worry of how could we know to what extent this 'naughtiness' is going to express itself. Is it going to be the child stealing a packet of Smarties from the newsagent, or is he going to get out his Kalashnikov and mow down a village of people? I don't think I'd want to abort on the off chance that it was the Kalashnikov and not the Smarties (*Start the Week*, 1995).

On being asked if her work sets out exclusively to explore male violence
My main source of thinking about how violence happens is myself, and in some ways all my characters are me. I write about human beings, and since I am one, the ways in which all human beings operate is feasibly within my understanding. I don't think of the world being divided up into men and women, victims and perpetrators. I don't think those are constructive divisions to make, and they make for very poor writing (Langridge and Stephenson, 1997).

On The Perceived Bleakness of Her Work

Probably all my characters in some way are completely Romantic. I think nihilism is the most extreme form of Romanticism, and that I think is where the plays get misunderstood. I think I'm a complete and utter Romantic, in the tradition of [John] Keats and Wilfred Owen (Tabert, 1998).

My plays certainly exist within a theatrical tradition, though not many people would agree with that. I'm at the extreme end of the theatrical tradition. But they are not about other plays; they are not about methods of representation. On the whole they are about love and about survival and about hope; and to me that is an extremely different thing (Rebellato, 1998).

Through being very, very low comes an ability to live in the moment because there isn't anything else. What do you do if you feel the truth is behind you? Many people feel depression is about emptiness but actually it's about being so full that everything cancels itself out. You can't have faith without doubt, and what are you left with when you can't have love without hate? (Benedict, 1996).

I don't find my own plays depressing or lacking in hope. But then I am someone whose favourite band is Joy Division because I find their songs uplifting.[63] To create something beautiful about despair or out of a feeling of despair is for me the most hopeful life-affirming thing a person can do. Because the expression of that despair is part of the struggle against it, the attempt to negate it (Thielemans, 1999).

Every time I let my cat out I think some vivisectionist is going to put washing powder in its eyes. I think that tends to indicate some kind of general depression about the state of the world. Well, doesn't it? (Stratton, 1998)

On Gender Politics

The journalist Rosie Boycott asked Kane if she was surprised by the negative critical reaction to Blasted, *and whether this* might have come from the fact that she was a young female dramatist exploring male violence.

No – it doesn't surprise me at all. The fact that it was written by someone in their early twenties who was a female I think exacerbated that critical anger. The violence that is being perpetrated in Bosnia is largely by fifteen- and sixteen-year-old boys rampaging throughout the country raping and pillaging. And the fact that someone who is outside of that could draw attention to it I think angered them (*Start the Week*, 1995).

I'm not writing about sexual politics. The problems I'm addressing are the ones we have as human beings. An over-emphasis on sexual politics (or racial or class politics) is a diversion from our main problem. Class, race and gender divisions are symptomatic of societies based on violence or the threat of violence, not the cause.

My only responsibility as a writer is to the truth, however unpleasant that truth may be. I have no responsibility as a woman writer because I don't believe there's such a thing. When people talk about me as a writer, that's what I am, not on the basis of my age, gender, class, sexuality or race. I don't want to be a representative of any biological or social group of which I happen to be a member. I am what I am. Not what other people want me to be (Langridge and Stephenson, 1997).

British Culture in the 1990s

Britart

Here, Nils Tabert asked Kane if she had seen a specific painting from the 1997 Saatchi Sensation *Exhibition. The painting in question was Marcus Harvey's portrait of serial killer Myra Hindley constructed out of children's palm prints. Entitled* Myra, *the painting became one of the most controversial of this high-profile exhibition. On plans to exhibit it at the Royal Academy several members of the board resigned and the actual painting itself was defaced by a member of the public soon after the exhibition opened. The picture was restored, but during its time in Britain was flanked by attendants.*

For the British tabloid press, the figure of Myra Hindley has always been a source of prurient fascination. Not surprisingly, Harvey's portrait became the subject of a series of hysterical articles in which calls for the painting to be banned and the parents of the child victims of Brady and Hindley called upon for their reactions to the portrait. Despite her life sentence, the press always chose to represent Myra Hindley through a photograph taken by the police immediately after her arrest in 1965. Harvey's portrait alludes to the ways in which the media have almost exclusively represented Hindley through this single image, more than forty years after the murders took place.

I didn't see it. I had very mixed feelings about it, because on the one hand I suppose I would defend anyone's right to create a piece of art out of anything they want; and yet somehow with the Myra Hindley picture . . . Without having seen it, I suspected that the artist's intentions were not entirely honest. I've always tried to avoid any reference to an actual situation. So, in *Blasted* I didn't want to mention Bosnia because then you get into an argument with people who were actually there and have experienced it. I've always thought that if you can avoid actual case histories but still write them then that's fine. What I wouldn't want to do is upset someone by reference to someone like Myra Hindley or a specific situation. Like *Cleansed*, I didn't want to get into the situation of: this is about Germany and the Jews. It definitely had a strong impact on me, but the play is not about that, so why use that to give something a context? Because then you're being cynical; you are using people's pain in order to justify your own work which I don't think is acceptable. Also, I think there's the problem that when you get so specific, something actually stops having resonance beyond the specific. As I've said, I haven't seen it, so I don't know whether the Myra Hindley picture has any resonance outside of the specifics of those children that were killed; and if it doesn't then it isn't justifiable because then you are just tapping in on a group of people who lost their kids – whereas I hope that *Cleansed* and *Blasted* have resonance beyond what happened in Bosnia or Germany specifically (Tabert, 1998).

Theatre
In the extract below Kane is asked if she believes that a renaissance has taken place in new British theatre writing during the mid 1990s.
No. I think what has happened in the English theatre is mainly because of Stephen Daldry.[64] There are more new plays produced in London now than in the past. Stephen has completely revolutionised the way of working at the Royal Court and has doubled the number of new plays being shown. If he had not done *Blasted*, it would not have been shown. I think the reason everyone is talking of a renaissance is that the critics think that all these plays are exceptional, but I say there are more because more are being shown (Giammarco, 1997).

Below Kane comments on her association with the youthful resurgence of new theatre writing in the mid 1990s.
I do not believe in movements. Movements define retrospectively and always on grounds of imitation. If you have three or four writers who do something interesting, there will be ten others who are just copying it. At the moment you've got a movement. The media look for movements, even invent them. The writers themselves are not interested in it. Some of the writers who are said to belong to this movement I haven't even met. So, as far as I am concerned, I hope that my play [*Crave*] is not typical of anything . . . Someone said to a Scottish playwright that you couldn't call his work [representative of the] 'New Writing,' because the play was not brutal enough. That is exactly the problem with movements, because they are exclusive rather than inclusive . . . When people come to see *Crave* they will be surprised; or they will find that the label does not apply. I do not consider myself a 'New Brutalist' (Thielemans, 1999).

1990s Scottish Playwriting

Opening at the Traverse [in Edinburgh with *Crave*] has probably been the highlight of my life. Three of my favourite writers
are David Harrower, David Greig and Chris Hannan: they
have a sort of lyricism and ambition. It might also be to do
with the fact that there are masses of writers produced in
London who get an absurd amount of national attention. I
always find it ridiculous that when I have a play on in London
the *Glasgow Herald* will come down and review it. I can't say I
notice the *Independent* rushing off up to review things in
Scotland. There is a complete imbalance in the press, which
means for example that Joe Penhall is better known than David
Greig, who is a far better writer. I also think that because there
are far more writers produced in London, there are inevitably
more bad ones. But then again when you think that three of the
best writers at the moment are all from Scotland, what's that
about? (Rebellato, 1998)

*Kane brings up the subject of London bias again in a piece of
her own journalism.*
Earlier this year, I was asked by *Time Out* to list the best ten
shows of the past 30 years. I made my list before realizing that,
of course, *Time Out* meant the best ten shows in the capital. I'd
seen only one of my ten in London. Cheek By Jowl's *Macbeth*
(Kane, 'The Only Thing I Remember Is', 1998).[65]

Working with Kane

Jo McInnes

Jo McInnes is an actress and director. She appeared in all three Royal Court productions of 4.48 Psychosis, *directed by James Macdonald. These included its premiere in 2000 and revival the following year. The American tour of 2004 lasted six weeks and included two new actors – one British (Jason Hughes) and one American (Marin Ireland). Other theatre work as an actress includes debbie tucker green's* dirty butterfly *(Soho Theatre, 2003), and David Eldridge's* M.A.D *(2004). Directing work includes Simon Stephen's* Christmas *(Bush, 2004).*

I'd like to ask about the reactions you got from critics and audiences to the American tour of 4.48 Psychosis.

When we worked on the play the very first time, we named each section with different things. The section, 'I am sad/I feel the future is hopeless and that things cannot improve' (206), we called 'The Assessment' because this kind of assessment was done a lot in 1950s America. However, the line 'I am sad' immediately got a huge laugh, whereas no one got the joke in London. I think in America many more people were laughing at themselves because they'd been through that whole culture of looking at yourself. Being able to be objective is not a British trait. Because we had an American actress playing an American it stopped anyone saying the play was about British people and had got nothing to do with them.[1]

In LA on the first night it was very bizarre. They didn't know what to think of it. And then we had this amazing review in the *LA Times* which opened everyone up to it.[2] The first two nights were very quiet – you couldn't hear any laughter. You could feel the fear. In *4.48 Psychosis* more than any other play I've known you're completely connected and open to the audience and what they're feeling. It's difficult to describe. You're not one on one with another actor – you're not looking into another actor's eyes – you're completely in communion with the audience. When you're doing it right, you open yourself to feel what the audience is feeling.

Do you think that the audience identify vicariously with the actor on-stage in some of those speeches such as, 'And I go out at six in the morning and start my search for you' (214). In a sense, do they project themselves into that search?

I think that's true. Audiences will say they know that pain because it's coming off from you. And then I'm getting their pain coming straight back at me. You feel people's sensitivity, people's rawness, people's openness and people who won't accept it – that also happens. You can't analyze it – it's just a feeling. I sometimes talked to Jason and Marin who did it with us in America, and said there were some nights when you would come away like you've never felt – completely *cleansed* with a love and joy of life. I find it an uplifting play to do. Other people find it an exhausting play. It's the same with audiences: some nights in New York, the audiences would come out and look as if they'd been on drugs. However, it can also be played so self-indulgently if you're not careful.

Did the American dimension take any other forms using British and American actors?

Not to me it didn't. A couple of Americans in Minneapolis felt it was odd hearing lines such as, 'What am I like'? (239). That's so quintessentially English, and it was always Marin the American actress who had to say them just by pure fluke. Marin had to ask what the phrase meant. But the play is so much bigger than nationality: it doesn't matter who's sat here, how old they are. People really got that in America.

Did you adopt the same approach as the Royal Court production by opening the shutters of the theatre at the end or finding an equivalent action?
We did that wherever we went. All of the theatres were different. Sometimes we could just walk out and go which was gorgeous. Some of the playing spaces were huge. The universities there have lots of money it seems; and we would often be playing on their main stage, but with the mirror and the audience all on-stage. The mirror was so much bigger for the American tour. We played to audiences of 250 to 300. So you would see hundreds of faces reflected in that mirror.

Did you have much time to rehearse the play again before going to America?
What James did was to work separately with Jason and Marin. They did a lot of reading of the books we'd read[3] and then we had two weeks with the three of us together.

Was it a replication of the two Royal Court productions?
Yes. James and I discussed this and it took us a long time to get there. And then it just becomes an exercise in doing it differently. It's for someone else to do. Our production was different because it's got different people in it – that very fact makes it different.

Did you find that the play placed any specific demands on you as an actor?
When you come off stage and you haven't delivered that play you feel like shit. Although *4.48 Psychosis* is a very free play, it's also like a piece of music. You have to learn the piece of music really well, then you can be free with it. It's like being in a band. You feel as if you're plugging your amplifier in and you're off!

It's an absolutely mammoth piece of work and I could do it at sixty and still be learning. Sometimes you feel that Sarah Kane's having a dialogue with you – she obviously understood acting extremely well. I think she's asking for a purity in you as an actor. I felt that by the end of those six weeks in America enriched in all sorts of ways.

Interview with Ian Rickson, 8 September 2005

Ian Rickson was artistic director of the Royal Court Theatre 1997–2007. His directing credits include Alice Trilogy *by Tom Murphy (2005),* The Sweetest Swing in Baseball *by Rebecca Gilman (2004),* Fallout *by Roy Williams (2003),* Not Not Not Not Not Enough Oxygen *by Caryl Churchill (1971, revival 2002), and* Dublin Carol *by Conor McPherson (2000). He also directed* The Weir *by Conor McPherson (1997–8), which transferred to London's West End in spring 1998 and premiered on Broadway in 1999, for which he was nominated Best Director at the 1999 Olivier Awards. His other directing credits include* The Day I Stood Still *by Kevin Elyot (1998),* Mojo *by Jez Butterworth (1996),* The Lights *by Howard Korder (1996) and* Pale Horse *by Joe Penhall (1995). In 2006 he directed Harold Pinter in* Krapp's Last Tape *and, in 2007, he directed the revival of Harold Pinter's* The Hothouse *at the National Theatre.*

The first thing I wanted to ask was your own thoughts about the 1994 season at the Royal Court that culminated in Blasted. Looking back there was a lot of energy being stored up: partly to do with the regime change at the Royal Court with Max [Stafford-Clark] departing and Stephen [Daldry] arriving – and partly to do with the interim arrangement, which was complex, where Max and Stephen worked together. But there was also an element of the theatre somewhat stalling in the period immediately before this point. Stephen was finding his feet and there was a sense of benign compromise in some of the programming.[4] For me personally there was a year between 1993 and 1994 of being stuck in the office desperately waiting to direct. At this time, there was a very unified view that in order to make an impact we had to get as many plays on as possible.

Stephen's good fortune was that Max had built up financial reserves plus the money from the commercial transfers of [Ariel Dorfman's] *Death and the Maiden* and [David Mamet's] *Oleanna*, meaning the company was quite cash rich.[5] Generally, the periods of creative fertility at the Court have tended to be at times when financial resources were good, because if you are going to do plays with the kind of quick turnaround of that first season you need a lot of money. Half a million pounds would be drawn down from reserves over the next three years, so I think there were several factors: financial, structural and artistic, in re-examining core values of the Royal Court.

Some of the plays we produced – for example [Joe Penhall's] *Some Voices* and *Blasted* – were not originally the Royal Court's. Sarah was at the Bush at the time [working as a Literary Assistant], and both of those plays had been passed on by the Bush, so one has to be careful about saying that the Royal Court 'invented x' or whatever. Theatres can have purposeful policies about putting work together, but nobody invents anything – the writer is the primary artist.

I can remember *Some Voices* and *Blasted* coming in on the same week and James Macdonald and I meeting Sarah in early 1994, doing readings of them on the same day and deciding who should direct what. I think initially we didn't value *Blasted* as highly as we do now. It took some encouragement from people like Caryl Churchill to give us the ultimate confidence to programme the play.

As for the whole season, you had *Some Voices*, [Rebecca Prichard's] *Essex Girls*, [Michael Wynne's] *The Knocky*, [Judy Upton's] *Ashes and Sand*, *Blasted* and [Judith Johnson's] *Uganda*. Looking back, I feel proud that there was a searching spirit of discovery, range and, with *Blasted* particularly, a kind of provocation. This was not chic or meaningless. It was a very felt, carefully prepared, politically reasoned provocation to do with contemporary society, and a terrible sense of corruption of our culture which drove through that play.

I'd like to ask about your decision when made artistic director to programme Cleansed *in the Theatre Downstairs.*

Cleansed was the first play I ever programmed when I took over as artistic director, and it was originally thought of as a Theatre Upstairs piece. There was another play programmed Downstairs, the nonetheless impressive *Gas Station Angel* by Ed Thomas, but I swapped them around. I hoped to make a defiant statement in launching the new season Downstairs. Can you imagine it now – *Cleansed* in the West End? It was on at the Duke of York's Theatre and I think one of the most expensive shows ever at the Royal Court with the budget going over considerably. Programming it came from the erratic confidence of the inexperienced or the naive, but I have some vestigial pleasure that we could do that – that we could put a play like that on in the West End.

What were your feelings towards the literary qualities in Kane's work? Did you pick up on these yourself?

I think less so early on, but I think particularly when *Crave* came in: those of us who knew T. S. Eliot for example could see the influences behind that play far more clearly. And then I guess going from that into *4.48 Psychosis*, which feels to me much more original: a really concerted attempt to search through feeling using form into somewhere really remarkable, difficult and searing. And perhaps here any influences simply fell away.

What were your reactions to the press attention given to Blasted?

On the one hand you feel heartened that a small sixty-seater house should have such impact; and that feels very encouraging when you worry that theatre is in danger of becoming the equivalent of croquet in British sports: i.e. that it doesn't mean much, is a bit rarefied and deeply unfashionable. To have something speaking to only fifty-seven people or however many the capacity was then, yet scorching its way on to the front pages and on to *Newsnight* is encouraging – playwriting suddenly has vitality. But I think at the same time we felt very under threat. We felt terrible for Sarah who felt hunted, and not understood which was upsetting. But when you look at the history of the Court it has always rallied when under threat, and it's often been strongest when it's against something. So the fact that it had the fortune to have this new play which really stirred up things, I think was a very good thing, but it wasn't pleasant at the time. There were tabloid journalists sneaking in, and Sarah at the time was only twenty-three so it wasn't good.

What were your recollections of the decisions made to stage the Sarah Kane retrospective at the Royal Court in 2001?
Firstly of course we had this play *4.48 Psychosis*, and we were really taking care to find the right conditions to present it such as not too near to her death or in any way to seem exploitative. Secondly there was a very strong feeling that her work as a whole had a distinctiveness, a formal boldness that really needed reappraisal and to be communicated to a wider audience. Also, a whole generation of people were aware of her work but hadn't seen it in performance. So it was a very good opportunity back in our home theatre after a period away to present a group of the plays together in a very purposeful season.⁶ Perhaps the plays were like a gauntlet thrown down to other writers, and to the critics, who to their credit did reappraise them more positively.

Of course, it's still difficult work to put on in England. They follow a long line of key plays at the Court including [John Arden's] *Serjeant Musgrave's Dance* and [Edward Bond's] *Saved* which may perform poorly at the box-office, but are really vital to the company's identity.

John Mahoney commented that the Royal Court, and especially Sarah Kane's plays risk the danger of becoming a 'brand' and so having a detrimental effect on new plays and playwrights emerging on the continent. How would you respond to such criticism?

The return to text in continental Europe over the past ten years is a phenomenal story. Almost all the major auteurs – Peter Brook, Luc Bondy, and Peter Stein, for example – have turned to new British plays. Part of the Royal Court's role is to be an international theatre, so we're much more concerned with *our* ability to pick up what is exciting abroad. I think we've done eight Russian plays in the last eight years as well as German and Brazilian plays – and that's our concern. If those continental auteurs want to do Kane then it's nothing to do with us. We're doing our own thing here and that's preoccupying enough!

Interview with Jeremy Weller, 23 March 2006

Jeremy Weller is artistic director of the Grassmarket Project, formed in Edinburgh during 1989. The company specialises in bringing together professional and non-professional actors to share their life experiences with an audience. The people often come from marginalised groups such as Brazilian street children and British young offenders. The performances are often characterised by their emotional intensity, the blurring between what is real and what is 'performed'.

When did you first become aware of Sarah Kane's work?
I read about *Blasted* when it first went to the Royal Court. And I thought this is just what is needed. This is someone who is actually doing what I think is important – actually getting down and dirty – and saying, 'this is what exists', but without being sensationalist about it. I actually thought the opposite of what most people did at the time in that it seemed to me that Sarah was dealing with the real stuff of life. I'd been in Kosovo [for the play *Soldiers*] and interviewed the tortured and the torturers, and all the stuff she dealt with in *Blasted* was just average. So that was when I became aware of her work – then I started to hear things that she was saying about me. Although I haven't deliberately marginalised myself, it's happened all the

same because I've always concentrated on the kind of theatre that interested me. I didn't really worry about what other people were doing. So it was strange to hear about a Royal Court writer mentioning me. Even though she was a very brilliant dramatist – and really pushing the boundaries – she was still what I considered to be more of a 'theatre person' doing traditional 'theatre writing'.

I found it interesting that while the so-called 'in-yer-face' group of writers with which Kane's been associated were mainly London based, Kane herself always seemed to have much more of an interest in what was going on in Scotland – not only with the Grassmarket Project but also other playwrights based there such as David Greig, David Harrower and Chris Hannan.

I think that's right. For example, I know that she went to the Edinburgh Festival every year. I think she saw it as a place where people like me could thrive because we didn't have the financial and pragmatic concerns of London and other major cities. We had freedom to develop as we pleased out of a hothouse atmosphere and out of the situation where you had to get a piece of theatre writing prepared for a run. People in the Festival were developing shows that could be more like an experience because there was no pressure for it to run longer than two or three weeks. So I think it created a kind of 'live' experience which Sarah sort of fed off – that edginess where you could take risks. However, saying that I think that if Sarah hadn't had the Royal Court she wouldn't have survived, because they nurtured her and allowed her to develop.

I gather that Sarah went to see five consecutive performances of Mad *when she visited The Edinburgh Festival. It's also been well documented that she believed those performances not only changed her life but also made her re-evaluate what theatre could achieve. However, I've argued elsewhere that there was always a conflict going on in Kane's own work, so that one part of her wanted those truly experiential moments that feature in*

your work where anything could happen . . .[7]
And often did!

So that one part of her wanted to break down that demarcation between 'the real' and ' the performed', while her writerly instincts always wanted to impose strict formal controls over the plays – and those two desires were never reconciled.
I think that's a very acute observation and I think that's probably where we divorced in our interests. For any given project, I write a lot and give it to both the non-actors and professional actors who are mixed in, but I'm also looking for that 'life' – the emotion – the rawness to be present. And I wouldn't want to imprison my people in the text. I wouldn't want to refine it to lyrical prose because I think that would squeeze out the life. Whereas I think you're right – and that Sarah had a love for the sacredness of the text and the mixing of the two. I know that was something we both spoke about, and I told her that theatre for me was a realm where you could explore life, but it had to be through other people's lives which would always have to supersede. You can give people text to perform and you can impose limits, but you have to give the performers their freedom.

I wanted to break down the suspension of disbelief. I wanted people to come to the theatre and believe totally. I've always wanted the audience to completely believe in the people they see in front of them – to believe that the emotions are real and that the actors are real. Yes, we're in the artifice of the theatre, but what you're seeing is as near to life as you can get. That excited Sarah as well.

One thing that struck me about Mad *was its focus on the confessional – that we were there as the audience to witness traumatic experiences, and that the performers were also on-stage with a need to confess something to the audience. It's something I've also noticed in Kane's drama, particularly so in her last two plays.*

That was another parallel thing that we both agreed on. The theatre is a domain where you can explore life and the inner workings of human beings to reveal some kind of truth. But art can actually run counter to that. If you move too much towards art, you can lose those inner workings. As far as *Mad*'s concerned it became a confessional because it was a play that dealt with mental illness. I interviewed a lot of people in secure units. Most of them had their illness to deal with, but also another thing which was the inability for others to understand what had happened to them. So the form of *Mad* came out of that, and the confessional was forced upon me by the women's experiences. So the form of the play and the end of the play is where the director on-stage says, 'I don't know if I felt something', because the actors confront him at one point and say, 'Did you feel anything today?' So I'm nailing my colours to the mast and saying that in theatre experience is everything. I think Sarah was also in the same boat. She was releasing all these demons into the world in order to say, 'This is what experience is like. Share this with me.'

On your meetings with Sarah Kane, were there any things that struck you about her ideas on theatre and performance?
She actually wrote in one of my notebooks, 'Let's wake those bastards up!' In my understanding of Sarah in the short time I knew her was the huge responsibility of the artist to wake people up to how things are. And she had that old-fashioned belief – as I do – that somehow the truth is worth telling, even if it's ugly.

How far did you agree with Kane's analysis of Mad *where she likened it to a form of catharsis in which the audience emerged inoculated against the world for a short while?*
I agreed with that. The nine women performers and the three actors wanted to share their experiences and the performances changed them. In a way going through all these people's sufferings and small joys had made them realise that they had gained a perspective on their own lives. So I think that the analogy of

an inoculation was true. Also, as an audience member you're honestly let into someone's inner world. I know that some people were affronted by it and I heard comments such as, 'I don't want that much information'!

Have you seen/read 4.48 Psychosis *?*
No, I avoided it, because on one occasion Sarah spoke to me about suicide because I asked. She said some very fundamental things that are not for this conversation out of respect; but some of the things she spoke about I've heard many times from young offenders, or people who've been in moments of raw experience such as the young boys who had been tortured in the Serbian prisons. I think that, in a sense, how she lived and the things she experienced contributed to her death.

Can you talk a little about the collaboration you had spoken about shortly prior to her death?
Our initial discussions were about taking the form of theatre that I work in and making Sarah the subject. She would be the subject matter of our show. She would be in it and the performance would be about her, and also about art and the suffering that artists undergo.

Would this have been in the form of a monologue or would other actors have been involved?
No. I saw it as just her on-stage. She liked that idea and said that she'd performed in productions of *Cleansed* and *Crave*.

Would she have distanced the narrative through 'acting' as another person?
No. It would have been taken directly from her own life.

Sarah has a reputation for being a 'writerly' dramatist in that her influences are mainly literary, but were there any theatre companies who specialised in non-textual drama who she ever spoke about?

No, I can't say she ever spoke about other companies that devised their own work as an ensemble. I think what attracted her to my work was the obsession I have about breaking the boundaries between what is 'real' on-stage and what is performed – to the point where the audience wants to actively intervene with the action on stage and shout, 'Stop it!' I remember in *Mad* the scene in which one of the women performers gets one of the male actors to play the part of her former boyfriend and enact out the violence she experienced at his hands. At first he feigns hitting her, and she says, 'No, you're not getting this right.' So she takes over and slaps him really hard. The scene ends with her kicking, punching and dragging him naked around the stage; and during that scene people in the audience actually cried out, 'Stop this!' And that was Sarah Kane's main interest in that people would want to stop something happening on stage because it was too real.

I also think that what Sarah liked about *Mad* was that it took the domestic and showed the real horror behind the doors in normal families. There are prisons and there are torture camps such as Guantanemo Bay, but there are also torture chambers in the E11 and SW1 districts of London, where a man comes home and tortures someone each evening in a domestic setting.

Interview with Aleks Sierz, 8 September 2005

Aleks Sierz is visiting research fellow at Rose Bruford College, and author of In-Yer-Face Theatre: British Drama Today *(2001) and* The Theatre of Martin Crimp *(2006). He also works as a journalist, broadcaster, lecturer and theatre critic.*

You have been one of the most honest critics of Sarah Kane's work and have commented on what you see as its shortcomings as well as the danger of the critical establishment adopting her as, in your own phrase, 'Saint Sarah'. What do you feel are the weaknesses in Kane's writing and the dangers of the elevated reputation she currently enjoys?

Well, the Saint Sarah thing was brought home to me in March 2005 when I went to the Sarah Kane Symposium at the Schaubühne in Berlin.[8] At the airport, I saw Graham Whybrow[9] and James Macdonald, the two apostles of Kanedom, and when I got to the theatre it was full of young women with short hair dressed in black – and I thought, 'Yes, it must be Easter because the pilgrims are gathering at the shrine of Saint Sarah'. Even now, I get a couple of emails a week about Sarah Kane from students wanting to know about her life and the way she died. Often their interest is prurient. I know it sounds very parental, but I really disapprove of her career path, the way she became increasingly subjective and increasingly suicidal in a theatrical as well as a literal sense. And I really loathe the way that some people see suicide as glamorous, and as validating a writer's life: Sarah Kane killed herself; therefore, she really meant it, whatever that 'it' was. Lots of other artists have struggled with form and content – think of Caryl Churchill or Martin Crimp – but without that sense of absolute control that Kane tried to impose both on her work and on her life. Control freaks are always suspect.

Dominic Dromgoole made a good point when he said, 'The only problem with Sarah, in my view, is that I'm not sure she's a natural writer',[10] and I can understand that perfectly. What he's suggesting is that she doesn't write easy dialogue. She's not the type of writer that, if you're making a soap opera, you'd immediately employ. With her, the dialogue isn't just dialogue, it always has another purpose – creating a stage image or advancing a certain case. It's not necessarily naturalistic: dialogue in the second half of *Blasted* certainly isn't, nor is it in *Cleansed*.

If you're going to criticise her work I think that you have to look at the writing itself. I did over-praise her when it mattered, when her work was in danger of being censored in the mid 1990s. However, since then I have reassessed some of her plays.

For example, for me the first half of *Blasted* is meant to be naturalistic, but if you actually read it line by line there's an uneasy mixture of Naturalism, in which the characteristic tone is 'Sarky little tart this morning, aren't we?' (26) and a more Beckettian style. For example, Ian's offhand comment, 'You have kids, they grow up, they hate you and you die' (21) is so polished, it's Beckettian. In real life, I don't think Ian could say that. Equally unnaturalistic is Kane's rewriting of *King Lear*, and of Beckett. So Hamm's line from *Endgame* about God – 'The bastard! He doesn't exist!'[11] – comes out as Cate saying, 'God' – and Ian replying, 'The cunt' (57). It's a strong, punchy line, but there's clearly more going on than just Naturalism.

I think that the success of the first half of *Blasted* comes from the fact that the psychology of the relationships and the characters are deeply and convincingly imagined, but there are occasional dissonant notes. For example, would somebody as shy as Cate really talk about masturbating?[12] I don't think so. In *Blasted*, not every line is perfectly successful. Like all great playwrights, Kane in 1995 was rewriting other writers, but she was also a beginner.

Martin Crimp seems to make a veiled reference to Sarah Kane's death in 'When the Writer Kills Himself', one of his 'Four Unwelcome Thoughts'. Do you see this as an implicit criticism, or is it just an observation?

You'd have to ask him. The piece is certainly a reference to Sarah Kane. I've used it a couple of times at theatre conferences as a way of breaking the ice, as a way of saying, 'Here is one writer commenting on the cult of another writer.' It's not actually commenting on Sarah's writing style, or on her impact on British theatre; he's commenting on the way people have turned her into an icon. Crimp's satirical prose pieces are always very sharp, partly because he talks about things that most writers don't talk about – such as professional jealousy and mutual suspicion. But he's right in that Sarah Kane *has* become an icon.[13] I remember Graham Whybrow once saying that with a really good writer, if you tore a page out of their play and threw it on the floor with a thousand other pages, you'd still be able to recognise their style from amongst all the other dialogue – and that's certainly true of Kane.

Talking of her as an icon, I typed 'Sarah Kane' into Google today and got 160,000 pages. And then you've got this paradox: she's frequently mentioned and frequently produced all over the world, but in Britain her work has only been put on at the Royal Court. Okay, there was also a production of *Blasted* and *4.48 Psychosis* at the Glasgow Citizens Theatre, but that are about it. No other productions until this year, when there's going to be productions of *Phaedra's Love* and *Cleansed*. So, in this country, she's the iconic, but invisible, in-yer-face playwright.

But her influence really is widespread. I'll give you a couple of examples. In October and November 2000, Holly Baxter Baine had a play called *Good-bye Roy* on as part of the Royal Court's Exposure season of young writers. And she said in the press release that her favourite writers were Bertolt Brecht and Sarah Kane. Baine was just fifteen years old. In February 2003, debbie tucker green put on her first play, *dirty butterfly*, at the Soho Theatre. In the last scene, there is this damaged young woman with blood running down her legs, which is a clear echo of Cate's last appearance in *Blasted*.

Even tangentially, the opening scene of Kevin Elyot's *Forty Winks* – which was at the Royal Court last year – featured a hotel room with a closed bathroom door that concealed the secret visitor. That was another homage to *Blasted*. There's also Kaite O'Reilly's *Peeling*, which was first at The Door in Birmingham in 2002, and shows a group of women talking about Euripides' *The Trojan Women*. At one point there's an incantation, and they say, in turn, 'Fire'; 'Smoke'; 'Pestilence' – then they all say: 'Men' (22). The characteristics of war are: 'Woman's body as battlefield'; 'Rape as a war tactic'; 'Mutilation as a reminder' (23). Such lines are clear echoes of *Blasted*, and a perfect example of Kane's work creeping into other writers' imaginations. So although her work hasn't been put on much here, there has obviously been this very powerful influence.

Your book In-Yer-Face Theatre: British Drama Today *provided a bold snapshot of a particular period in British theatre history. However, do you think that now the book has the same problem as Martin Esslin's* Theatre of the Absurd, *when the term came back to haunt him? Also, do you feel that five years on from its publication your assessment of some of the writers from that period has been accurate?*

When I wrote the book, it was conceived as a polemic and a defence of a group of young writers. And it seemed really important to defend them. That was especially true in the mid 1990s. Soon after 1999, when Sarah Kane killed herself, a lot of the steam went out of that whole explosion of talent and many of the writers that I wrote about had become quite accepted. Publishing takes a while, and the book – in one sense – came out after its work in the real world had already been done. So I was defending Sarah Kane retrospectively. Since then, the problem has been over-praise of Kane rather than defending Kane.

However, when I was writing the book and thinking of its structure I was taking a punt on the future because when I decided to write chapter-length studies of Anthony Neilson, Sarah Kane and Mark Ravenhill there was no way of knowing whether they would keep on writing or whether they would remain as central as they were in the mid 1990s. With some of the other writers I made a mistake. Simon Block has faded away, as has Nick Grosso and Richard Zajdlic. Rebecca Prichard hasn't had a play staged for years.[14]

With Sarah Kane, however, I think I was triumphantly vindi-cated because not only was she an important new voice indi-vidually, but she was also a theatre practitioner who represented a whole sensibility. Like all writers, she wasn't happy to be co-opted as part of a movement. When I told her that I was writing a book called *In-Yer-Face Theatre*, she just gave a characteristic shrug as if to say, 'That's your problem mate, not mine'! And then added, 'At least it's better than fucking New Brutalism'! But I've never seen in-yer-face theatre as a movement. I see it as a sensibility, and there's a big difference. I must say that one of the more pertinent criticisms of the book is that I was too inclusive by including too many different writers under the same label. I think that the brand 'in-yer-face' applies to Kane's work very well; because it conjures up that sense of immediacy and rawness, which is an essential part of her artistic personality, and it also refers to the relationship between audience and stage. The whole point of the idea of 'In-Yer-Face Theatre' is that it doesn't just refer to a play's content; it's all about what's happening between the audience, the actors and the writer. And her idea of experiential theatre – which I illustrate by saying that it involves leaning forward in your seat, as opposed to speculative theatre, where you lounge back in your plush velvet throne and practically nod off – sums up her theatrical project very well. I think that time has vindicated the fact that she was an in-yer-face writer and that the label is meaningful in that it does describe a particular way of making theatre which became incredibly popular in the mid 1990s.

What do you feel about the perception that Kane became absorbed into the so-called 'lads' plays of the 1990s, and her own implicit endorsement by refusing to align herself to a female tradition of playwriting?

That's a good question. I think that she distanced herself from a whole collection of women writers because of their ideological feminism, and she realised two things: that ideological feminism was a thing of the late 1970s and early 1980s, and that it didn't really make much sense to young women living in the so-called post-feminist age. In other words, she could stand up for herself without leaning on an ideology. Simultaneously, I think she also understood that ideology makes for bad playwriting, and she wanted to distance herself from writers such as Sarah Daniels, Timberlake Wertenbaker and April de Angelis because they wrote with an agenda, and they were giving a target audience – usually other middle-class women – rather easy answers and rather easy emotional trajectories, whereas Kane preferred to tell audiences, both male and female, the bad news and present a reality that was difficult to live through. She believed in the modernistic project of putting you through hell so that you understood the world outside the theatre better, rather than in reconciling you with your innate prejudices.

Now, that's not to say that Kane didn't have a sexual politics. It's startlingly clear, and very troubling, that *Blasted* makes the connection between domestic rape and the use of rape as a war tactic. And the reason why I think it's troubling is that I don't believe it's either true or useful. In other words, if you ever met someone who's just been raped domestically and tell her that it's the same thing as being raped in Bosnia it's unlikely to be of any use to that person. And simultaneously, when dealing with rape victims in a war situation, it probably doesn't help to tell them that all men are potential rapists. But, irrespective of what I believe, this is still an example of sexual politics.

One of the results of Kane's raw and in-yer-face style was that people didn't examine her ideas closely enough. So, for example, David Greig in the introduction to her *Complete Plays* talks about *Blasted*, and he says: 'Her simple premise, that there was a connection between a rape in a Leeds hotel room and the hellish devastation of civil war, had been critically misunderstood as a childish attempt to shock' (x). And he's quite right about that, but, actually, what's interesting now is to move on and interrogate that premise. Is it true, and if it isn't true how does Kane get away from discussing it, avoid reasoning about it, by using her theatrical technique? I would always argue that because Kane was a moral absolutist, and believed there were no shades of grey, only black and white – and because she was a vigorous exponent of experiential theatre – what she habitually does is impose her ideas on the audience in an autocratic way which leaves no room for argument. Sometimes, an artist's fierce passion can be an imposition.

Isn't that as bad as the didactic dramatists she's trying to oppose?

Maybe. That's the irony of the serpent eating its own tail – the critique of didactic theatre goes full circle.

Critics have often commented on the difficulty of her stage directions. For instance, Ken Urban has spoken about the cruellest scene of her work being in Cleansed *where Robin has to consume two layers of chocolates from a box.*[15] *Phyllis Nagy however has commented that Kane needed to take responsibility for the stage actions she creates rather than dismissing these as someone else's problem.*[16] *What are your thoughts about the theatricality in her work?*

Plainly, she understood theatricality in a very intuitive and extremely intelligent way. That scene from *Cleansed* – I saw the original production by James Macdonald, which was cruel but quite brief. When I saw the Schaubühne production in March 2005, that scene took ages. The box of chocolates was enormous. The actor had to literally eat every single chocolate. Some were crammed in his face; others were thrown on the floor; others were kicked across the stage; he was forced to eat like a dog, like a woman, like a child – all different ways. It was excruciating, and because it was so drawn out it became physically unpleasant; yet also incredibly strong – a revenge on sentimental love. So I would always defend Kane's stage directions from the point of view of whether they work or not. And this scene does.

I once described the last scene of *Phaedra's Love* as risible, and that's because, when I saw it at the Gate Theatre, it was.[17] People weren't taking it seriously, partly because of the explicitness of the violence. It's very difficult to do gonad roasting and penis slicing in a way that inspires horror rather than derisory laughter. And it isn't just that the laughter is a barrier between us and ghastly feelings. The audience knows that there are no real body parts, and somehow you have to work so hard to convince them that there are, that perhaps an indirect approach – like the 'rats' used by James Macdonald and Jeremy Herbert in *Cleansed* – is a better way around it.

I thought that Jeremy Herbert's design solutions in that production were spot on. There was that scene where flowers are meant to appear from the ground (133). In fact, these rained from the ceiling. And as they came raining down, they hit the floor, and because they were all tipped with darts to stick in place you heard this thump, thump, thump of darts. Somehow, the contrast between the softness of flowers and the harshness of darts created a picture of love, pain and wonder – so an impossible stage direction was creatively realised. In contrast, the *Cleansed* I saw at the Schaubühne dispensed with all of those stage directions. It had no flowers; it was barren.

I once heard Martin Crimp say that some of Samuel Beckett's stage directions are brilliant, but some of them are really naff. So, Mouth in *Not I* is really brilliant, but The Auditor standing next to her, in a cloak, gesticulating, sometimes simply doesn't work.[18] So as long as the Beckett Estate polices the work and forces directors to include The Auditor, it's a bad thing. So I would always defend Sarah Kane's stage directions, but I would also give the director the freedom to dispense with the ones that they felt didn't work. By all means listen to what the writer is saying, but if you can't afford a vulture for *Phaedra's Love*, or having a shadow of a vulture doesn't work, or is just a distraction – well, cut it out.

What do you consider the current state of play regarding Sarah Kane's work?
I've got something to say which occurred to me after 9/11 and the London bombings. Now, after those events, when suddenly the word 'Muslim' was on everybody's lips, it's interesting to re-read the story of how *Blasted* came to be written. In the text itself, and in Kane's recorded interviews about the play, there's a gap – a silence – an absence of the dreaded word 'Muslim'. Although the play was inspired by massacres in Bosnia (which means Muslim), and Kane was haunted by the image of a

Bosnian woman (which means Muslim) hanging in a forest, the actual word 'Muslim' doesn't occur at all in the play. After 9/11 and after 7/7, this absence is much more noticeable than ever it was before. It's also interesting that Thomas Ostermeier's production of the play at the Schaubühne in 2005 tried instinctively to redress this by using a constant CNN news commentary about the Iraq war on the hotel television. Iraq, of course, is widely perceived by many Muslims as an anti-Muslim war.

Last but not least, *Blasted* is set in Leeds, which by an amazing coincidence – or was it a visionary prescience? – was the home of three out of the four 7/7 London bombers. But if Muslims are absent from *Blasted*, what's present is Ian's racism – part of which is explicitly directed at Pakistanis (once again read Muslim) – and that suggests that Kane understood the politics of racism and Muslim disaffection – partly unconsciously perhaps – quite a bit before it became such an important part of our political agenda.

I'll give you another example. When *Blasted* was first staged a Reverend Bob Vernon in a letter to the *Guardian* defended the play by pointing out that 'My local shopping centre looks like Grozny, only two out of two dozen shops remain'.[19] Once again, the mention of Grozny is a reminder of another anti-Muslim war, this time in Chechnya.

And critic Benedict Nightingale, when the play was restaged at the Royal Court in 2001, felt that Kane's moral, social and political vision reminded him of another political play, J. B. Priestley's *An Inspector Calls* (1947). Now you know very well that that play has an amazing line at the end when Inspector Goole lectures the audience that if they don't learn the lesson of social responsibility, 'they will be taught it in fire and blood and anguish'.[20] Well, in July 2001 about two or three months after that production, riots broke out in Burnley, Oldham and Leeds after Muslim youths were provoked by British National Party racists.[21] So once again, Kane's play becomes more resonant because of what was happening, and especially as regards what's been happening to Muslims.

There's another interesting thing. We've already spoken about the centrality of rape in Kane's vision of war. I remember that in her interview with you she was talking about the fact that the Vietcong didn't use rape in their war. So it's not something that is used in every war, only in specific wars such as the conflict in Yugoslavia. And in that interview she actually said the dreaded word 'Muslim'. So this 'Muslim Other' is invisible but present in her work, usually disguised by the word 'Bosnia'. As you know, her epic journey from the first draft and the first production you saw in Birmingham, to the final canonical text, was a process of excising specific cultural references and universalising the text. One of the things that she cut were local references to Gordon's Gin (substituting 'gin') and another was local names like 'Vladek' (substituting 'the Soldier'). So she was constantly moving between a specific struggle – the Bosnian war – and a more universal idea of war.

I'll leave this finally as a question. My point would be that this movement towards greater universality is obviously a good thing in terms of drama. You think of Beckett's universality, which means that his work can be reinterpreted in hundreds of different ways. It's writing for the future, but I would ask whether something is not also lost, and in particular whether the Muslims have been obliterated from that play? And that's important since if it hadn't been for the sufferings of Muslims that play would never have existed – it was Kane's response to their condition that provoked *Blasted* in the first place. In this way, art and reality exist in a twisted symbiosis.

* * *

Sarah Kane Symposium (1). The Pit: Barbican Centre, 11 November 2006

Panel
'Acting Kane'

Chair
Aleks Sierz

Contributors
Diana Kent *is an actress whose work for theatre includes David Edgar's* The Prisoner's Dilemma *(RSC, 2001), Bernard Marie-Koltès's* Roberto Zucco *(RSC, 1997) and J. B. Priestley's* An Inspector Calls *(RNT, 1992). Films include* Billy Elliot *(2000),* The Wings of a Dove *(1997),* Heavenly Creatures *(1994),* Morlang *(2001) and* Brothers of the Head *(2005). She played the eponymous role in Anne Tipton's 2005 production of* Phaedra's Love.

Suzan Sylvester *is an actress whose work for theatre includes Shakespeare's* Pericles *(RSC, 1990), Vassily Sigarev's* Black Milk *and the Presnyakov Brothers'* Terrorism *(both Royal Court, 2003). In 1988, Sylvester won an Olivier Award for Most Promising Newcomer in a revival of Arthur Miller's* A View from the Bridge *(Aldwych Theatre, 1987). She played the role of Grace in the 1998 Royal Court production of* Cleansed.

Dave Tool *is an actor and dancer, appearing in DV8's* Can We Afford This (the Cost of Living) *(live performance 2000; film 2004) and Sally Potter's film* The Tango Lesson *(1997). He played the Soldier in Graeae's 2006–7 production of* Blasted.

Aleks Sierz: *Clearly the work of Sarah Kane is challenging and strenuous for audiences and actors alike. If her demands on directors can be summed up by the famous stage direction in* Cleansed, *'The rats carry* **Carl's** *feet away' (136), her challenge to actors is equally knotty. At the end of* Blasted *Ian, according to Kane, 'dies with relief' (60). Now, you could try this at* *home: get an actor, give them that stage direction and watch their faces drop!*

I thought I'd start by asking the panellists to go through their experiences chronologically in terms of the plays, so Dave could you tell us about how you were chosen to play the Soldier in Blasted.

Dave Tool: I was originally asked by the director Jenny Sealey to read for the part of Ian. I didn't really know Sarah Kane's work at all. At first I really wanted to do it, but the more I thought about it I became less convinced and in the end I bottled out of it.

AS: *What made you bottle out?*

DT: Scaring the public by taking my clothes off – it was that mainly! Then I was asked if I'd read for the part of the Soldier instead. In the end, I was quite glad – it's fifteen minutes of pure magic.

AS: *Diana – with the role of Phaedra, how did you get cast for that?*

Diana Kent: Maggie Lunn, who was casting director at the RSC for one of the seasons I did there was also doing the casting for *Phaedra's Love* so that's how I was brought in. When I was at the RSC I also did a production of *Roberto Zucco* by Bernard Marie-Koltès, directed by James Macdonald. Not only is there a similarity in the writing between Koltès and Kane, but James also told me that Kane was a great fan of Koltès's work. The two plays are not dissimilar in terms of their strangeness in depicting human character.

AS: *Suzan – how did you get to* Cleansed?

Suzan Sylvester: I'd worked with James Macdonald a few times before on Chekhov's *The Seagull* [Sheffield Crucible, 1989] and Shakespeare [*Love's Labour's Lost*, Sheffield Crucible, 1992], and he asked me to come in to read for the play. I hadn't seen *Blasted*, but I'd heard all about the reviews and the public outcry. I went along to the Duke of York's to meet James and Sarah. I'd read the play. To me it was like an opera or a ballet, although I did see it as something quite small scale – something that could go on at the Theatre Upstairs, but we actually did it at the Duke of York's which is a massive space. It was quite a short meeting. I went in and was quite embarrassed because I was wearing black boots, combat trousers and one of those khaki army t-shirts with a red star and saw that Sarah was dressed in exactly the same way. I felt that I'd been following her around the streets! She was very quiet.

AS: *Let's talk about rehearsals. Dave, take us through the rehearsals of Graeae's* Blasted.
DT: I have to explain a little bit about Graeae theatre company for those who don't know their work. Graeae is a company which uses disabled actors with either physical or sensory disabilities. They're very involved in making productions that are accessible to all members of the audience. So we went into rehearsals knowing that we had to present this play in a way that would communicate with everyone. Luckily, the way the play is written a lot of the stage directions could be used as dialogue because in the opening of *Blasted* it says these lines could be used as dialogue for the actors (2).[22] So, for your visually impaired audience we had something there to work with – and for the actors it gave us the challenge of how we were going to present these stage directions. Do we present them neutrally or within the character as you're working? After some discussion, we decided that we'd keep them within the character – so you can emphasise certain stage directions such as '*He dies with relief*' (60).

AS: *What did you discover about the character of the Soldier during rehearsals?*
DT: This character has gone through so much in the war. His girlfriend's been raped and murdered by soldiers and he's done the same. You have to think how you're going to get to that

point. But then something happens where it gets to a point where it doesn't mean anything anymore.

AS: *I remember you telling me that you had three speeches which are basically about atrocities that have happened and the different ways you tried them out.*

DT: There's one speech in particular where the Soldier talks about going to a house where he finds these kids and one of them is taken outside by soldiers and shot while the other twelve-year-old girl is raped by the Soldier. In rehearsal, we presented the speech in a variety of ways. We even tried it as the Soldier telling the incident as a secret joke to Ian and as he was telling it really enjoying the experience. That worked, but we pulled it back and made the delivery quite flat. This made the tone more sinister because there was nothing going on in the character's eyes. That approach was stronger because he wasn't showing any emotion, so when it came to the part where the Soldier breaks down you could build to the point where he cracks and explodes.

AS: *Diana, what did you learn about Phaedra's passions in rehearsals?*

DK: I think *Phaedra's Love* is probably the simplest out of the plays in the sense that it's not baffling – you understand the story as you read it, whereas with the other plays it's more of a challenge to understand at first what's actually taking place. In *Phaedra's Love* it's the emotional journey and the emotional polarities that are the things you have to come to grips with. I knew that this would be very exposing, but I didn't think it would be as harrowing as it was because of the collision between Phaedra's desire for Hippolytus and how badly she is rejected – both by Hippolytus and the audience. So she starts out on a journey of salvation to save Hippolytus but this ends in her destruction.

AS: *Suzan, the character of Grace in* Cleansed *is a very complex role. How did you find your way through it in rehearsals?*

SS: Well, I'm not sure I did quite honestly. There was so much to take in. *Cleansed* felt like a piece of music in that it's got an internal rhythm that you have to judge within yourself when it's going out of synch. I got very overwhelmed with it and coped by thinking of each scene in pieces rather than the over-all play. I also think that with the production we did of *Cleansed* the feel of the play was very stark and sterile. We were also very distanced from the audience working in a larger theatre. What audience we had were further away so you didn't feel that connection. There was also a lot of physical theatre and the production was also very precisely designed so there wasn't any room for fuzzy edges, so that made me quite tense.

AS: Cleansed *is quite an ambiguous text, but when you're play-ing a line you can't play it ambiguously can you?*
SS: Precisely. You get lines like 'Definitely/If/But' (127), and behind each word there's a different meaning, or possibly two or three different meanings. So, it was difficult trying to find an emotional truth behind such seemingly static lines. Usually when you have more words you can sort of spread out your feelings. I also had the added difficulty of the director and Sarah saying 'do anything you want'! Sarah and Harold Pinter respected each other very much and Harold uses that same technique of using one or two words to describe so many different feelings.

AS: *Did it help to have Sarah in the rehearsals?*
SS: Quite honestly no. However, I didn't not want her to be there. Usually it's something of a responsibility to have the writer in rehearsals when you're trying to work your way through something, but Sarah didn't interfere in that way. It was more that she was watching what we were doing with James and the designer, and they worked very much as a three-some on the concept of the whole thing.

AS: *Dave. How did you respond to the male rape scene in* Blasted?

DT: I came to terms with the scene pretty quickly. What we decided on was that the rape scene wasn't going to be based on a traditional scenario: here I was going to use my leg to rape Ian. The practicalities were the biggest problem.

AS: *There was also another difficult moment when you suck out Ian's eyes. In the Graeae production, the actor playing Ian is partially sighted and you decided not to use any props.*
DT: The decision not to use props was made very early on. The stage we used was like a miniature cut-off skateboard bowl and so using props in that environment looked out of place. The other concern related to this was the issue of access for the audience. We had sign language interpreters on screen via video, and each character in the play had their own interpreter which creates different atmospheres within each scene – so for example you effectively have two different Soldiers threatening Ian even though the second Soldier is not physically on-stage. This also affected the rehearsal process because we had to get that done in the first one or two weeks; so we had to know the whole of the play in order to film these sign language sequences. By the time we got to the end of the rehearsals the pacing had changed slightly due to the presence of the video which could feel plodding at times.

Regarding the eye-sucking scene: because we actually spoke the stage directions as we performed them I was aware that I was getting closer and closer to an actor who was visually impaired and he was understandably nervous – at times, I actually physically sucked one of his eyes.

* * *

Sarah Kane Symposium (2). The Pit: Barbican Centre, 11 November 2006

Chair
Dan Rebellato is Professor of Contemporary Theatre at Royal Holloway, University of London.

Contributors
Mel Kenyon is Sarah Kane's agent.
Jens Hilje is literary manager at the Schaubühne Theatre in Berlin.
Graham Saunders is a lecturer in Theatre Studies at the University of Reading.
Maja Zade was previously senior reader at the Royal Court. In 2000, she joined the Schaubühne Theatre in Berlin as a dramaturge.

Dan Rebellato: *We'll be talking in this final session about Sarah Kane the writer. We'll be discussing not only the impact she made on the theatre that she emerged into during the mid 1990s, but also the kind of theatre that she has left behind. Mel, I'd like to start by asking you to assess the importance of* Blasted.
Mel Kenyon: Part of the reason I love *Blasted* and part of the reason why the (mainly) male critics (with one or two notable and very fine exceptions) hated the play was the emotional honesty with which Sarah had written the work; oddly her perspective on violence comes from a writer with a very robust style which is almost masculine, but at the same time I think possibly only a woman could have written with that passionate understanding and abhorrence of violence – and that comes from a very female perspective i.e. there's no glorification or gratuitous violence at all in *Blasted*: it's almost puritanical in its loathing of what Ian does to Cate, and what trauma has done to the Soldier. So when the critics accused her of gratuitous violence I thought, 'You stupid bastards – that's exactly what she

hasn't done, but you haven't seen this before.' And yet the critics were praising *Killer Joe* down the road, written by a male playwright Tracy Letts, in which of course a rape victim falls in love with her rapist – that's what girls do . . .[23]

DR: *Jens, I wonder if anything in Mel's description of that first encounter with* Blasted *chimes with your experience of encountering Kane's work? I'm also wondering what German theatre and specifically playwriting was like when it discovered Sarah Kane?*

Jens Hilje: If you recall, *Blasted* emerged in the mid 1990s so this took place after 1989 and the fall of the Berlin Wall. For about two years in Germany there was a kind of euphoric feeling that something could change – now there's going to be a free society for all of us. However, after two or three years the war started in Yugoslavia – a neighbouring country to Germany in which we saw civilisation collapse. Germany also had the same government it had twelve years before, so our country in many ways had remained completely the same.[24]

And it was the same in the theatre. There was a generation who had grown up in the post-1968 generation who were in a position of power in the theatre. The playwrights of the 1970s and 1980s such as Peter Handke and Heiner Müller were still the governing gods of the theatre scene and so everything was stuck completely. The only revolution there had been was in the aesthetics at the Volksbühne in Berlin in terms of acting and directing. It did this through an attitude – and the attitude was one of a deep, angry and profound cynicism. But after the mid 1990s, this attitude of cynicism began to feel its desperate emptiness in politics, theatre and fine art.

What happened with the plays that came from Britain such as Sarah Kane's *Blasted* and Mark Ravenhill's *Shopping and Fucking* was a kind of artistic weapon against cynicism. We knew that the new plays were infused with the British tradition of realism, but what realism is about is not a process of seeing and describing real life but an attitude that shows an awareness that behind the realism lurks deep pain and ignominy. So what came back to German theatre with those two British writers were those feelings – so that was a revelation for a whole new generation of German directors, playwrights and actors. It was a kind of different attitude towards a system that didn't work any more in theatre or politics.

DR: *It's interesting that Jens says* Blasted *was immediately recognised as responding to the collapse of the former Yugoslavia and that the play was itself seen as idealistic, because in Britain it was perceived as exactly the opposite, as a politically vague and theatrically cynical exercise. Maja, thinking about the intimate relationship you've enjoyed with translating Kane's work, do you have any general thoughts on what is translatable?*

Maja Zade: I didn't actually translate the plays. When Marius translated *Crave*[25] I helped him with trying to work out the meaning of some of the English lines. I was also production dramaturge on *4.48 Psychosis*, where we did some work on the translation. I think with plays like *Crave* and *4.48 Psychosis* the language is close to poetry and words are often repeated and varied slightly, but they refer back to where they were used before – so it's important to maintain that link. And sometimes it's a link by sound or association. Also it's a fact that in English a word can have several meanings and the meaning is decided by the sentence around it, whereas in German the words are very precise so they don't have the same ambiguity. You have to make choices when you translate it, which of course then leads to problems because sometimes you can't mirror the word before – you have to choose between the meaning and the sound in that particular sentence. A couple of times we 'phoned up James Macdonald because we needed someone who'd worked on the original production to try and help us when confronted with several choices. So, for example, we could ask him if rhythm or sound were more important than a particular meaning.

MK: Can I interject? It didn't come about very quickly. Although one or two critics championed her early work, I think I'm right in remembering this, Graham, that it wasn't until *Crave* that the critics thought she could actually write.

Graham Saunders: It's true. The irony is that *Crave* is a far more allusive and experimental play than *Blasted*, but critics felt more confident in understanding it because there were recognisable references to literary sources such as T. S. Eliot's *The Wasteland*, so they interpreted the play as belonging to a familiar strand of high modernism.

Blasted, despite starting off in a recognisable milieu of socio-realism, ends up disregarding the form entirely. Saying that, there are many clues in the first part that allude to the second such as Cate's fits, as well as the opening stage direction, '*a very expensive hotel room in Leeds – the kind that is so expensive it could be anywhere in the world*'(3). So there are big signposts in *Blasted* that alert you to the fact that things aren't quite what they seem.

MK: I also think that the inherent lyricism of *Crave* fooled the critics into thinking it was a 'feminine' and happy play from Sarah Kane, whereas I think it's perhaps her most deeply depressing and bleakest play. I find it even bleaker than *4.48 Psychosis*.

GS: That bright light at the end of *Crave* can be interpreted in many different ways. So it can be seen as indicative of a state of happiness or visions of angels, yet it could also be seen as all of the characters embracing a collective annihilation.

DR: *I remember her once telling me that she thought* Cleansed *was her happiest play. We've mentioned the growing recognition that Kane had emerged as a new and distinctive voice, but I'd like to ask Graham what he thinks constitutes the originality of Kane's work as a writer.*

GS: I think the originality shows in various ways. Certainly, she was innovative in terms of showing what the theatre could do. We heard earlier in the symposium from the actors about the sort of challenges she sets them as performers. She also does the same in terms of the challenges she sets for stage and lighting designers. The other thing about Kane's work is that each new play adopts a new dramatic form which is never repeated in the next play. I think she was also important in being a passionate advocate for the theatre itself above other media such as film or television.

MK: I also think that the work appeals to audiences in their late teens and early twenties partly because they can actually feel the plays rather than intellectualise them. With Sarah's work you can feel the psyche not in the sense of the spiritual well-being of the writer, but you do get a sense of something. Her work communicates that in a very direct way, so I think that a lot of people fall in love with the plays because they connect to them directly through the emotions.

JH: The interesting thing about the discussion we've been having here the whole day is that in Britain there still seems to be this debate about whether she is a good writer or not. In Germany nobody questions this anymore. In Britain, I still feel that you have to defend her as being an important writer. For example, Thomas Ostermeier's production of *Crave* is still running in repertoire after six years to packed-out audiences. She's also not considered to be a cynical writer, but someone who was able to express a truth that became visible in the 1990s which was all about the authenticity of the body after all other hopes have failed. It was all about the individual – you and your body and the ability to actually feel something which would give life meaning. This is why there is so much in her plays about hurting and mutilating the body. There are also these big themes in her work about the search for love and the return of war – these also became two of the big themes that defined the 1990s and she was one of the first to reflect these ideas in her plays.

DR: *I'm wondering if that became more apparent in Germany, because even though you're describing the post-1968 generation as dinosaurs still hanging on to power, nonetheless in a situation where Heiner Müller is still regarded as a central*

playwright, is Sarah Kane likely to be more easily understood?
MZ: In German theatre, there isn't the dominance of Natural-ism as there is in Britain. I think that's a big factor in explain-ing why she was more easily accepted. People in Germany expect to see big philosophical issues grappled with on-stage and often in a non-naturalistic way. I think that's why the audi-ences there were quick to take and accept the plays as being great work maybe.

DR: *Do you think that the recommendation she made to Thomas Ostermeier to stop producing British playwrights and start developing the work of dramatists in Germany has been followed up? And has her own work influenced the next gener-ation of German playwrights?*
MZ: A lot of people claim that writers such as Sarah Kane and Mark Ravenhill produced this whole new generation of Ger-man playwrights, and in a way that's true because they paved the way for new plays in German theatres, but I don't think they actually had any direct influence on those playwrights. So, Marius for example didn't know *Blasted* when he wrote *Fireface*. You had a parallel situation where these new plays were beginning to be written but also an incredible sense of frustration because their plays were not being produced because directors at the time were making a name for them-selves by deconstructing the classics. In Germany, it was not the done thing to direct new plays – that's not how you made your reputation. Then Thomas Ostermeier came along and directed all these new English plays which got other people interested – and then Peter Zadek directed the first German production of *Cleansed*. And so this in turn helped the new generation of German playwrights who were emerging at the same time.
MK: I also think the German theatres became more writer friendly. There was a time when writers were not welcome in the rehearsal room, so that after delivering their play the process became hermetically sealed – somebody cracked the play open and tinkered with it, adding new lines and taking away others

and the playwright was excluded from the whole process.

MZ: It's true. At the time, there was this enormous division between playwrights and theatres. Playwrights at the time sent their work directly to agents rather than the theatres who often didn't read unsolicited plays. What the Baracke theatre in Berlin did, and which has really changed the way that German theatres now work, is to get directly in contact with the writer. Whereas before there were hardly any playwrights in residence, now most medium-sized theatres have a relationship with a playwright, so the landscape has changed.

DR: *Mel and Graham – do you think Sarah Kane's work has had any impact or influence on British theatre or playwriting?*
MK: Well, I think if you're a really good playwright you're unique. So, while I'm sent some derivative Kane-inspired plays, they don't have the sensibility of that unique writer which makes the work so special. I think what happened – and Sarah is part of that – is that writing is now viable. In the 1980s playwriting wasn't seen as a viable way of earning a living, nor was it seen as a viable means of expression to anyone under the age of fifty. What 1994 did was that it opened the doors to a whole new generation of playwrights.[26] I think the emotional courage shown by Sarah and the other young writers of that generation has had a very good effect.

GS: I'd briefly just agree and add that the so-called 'in-yer-face' generation made playwriting 'cool' again. Whether the current generation of playwrights have embraced Sarah Kane's ambition and sense of experimentation I'm slightly more sceptical about. Whereas Sarah in terms of dramatic form blows up the hotel room in *Blasted*, the current generation seem to be going back into the room and rebuilding it.

Notes

PREFACE

1 Simon Hattenstone, 'A Sad Hurrah', *Guardian Weekend*, 1 July 2000.
2 Simon Stephens, Interview with Mel Kenyon, *Royal Court Sarah Kane Season: Information Pack*, 2001, p. 14.
3 Michael Billington, 'The Good Fairies Desert the Court's Theatre of the Absurd', *Guardian*, 20 January 1995.
4 Roger Foss, *What's On*, 25 January 1995.

CHAPTER 1

1 Stanley Wells and Gary Taylor (eds), *William Shakespeare, The Complete Works* (Oxford, 1988), p. 1184.
2 Alan Chadwick, Review of *Blasted*, *Metro*, 11 March 2002.
3 See Dominic Dromgoole, *The Full Room: An A–Z of Contemporary Playwriting* (London, 2000), p. 163; Aleks Sierz, 'A Review of *Complete Plays* by Sarah Kane', *Contemporary Theatre Review*, vol. 13, no. 1 (2003), 115–17.
4 *Newsnight Review*. Broadcast BBC 2, 6 April 2001.
5 John Mahoney, 'Blasted Theory', *Guardian*, 25 October 2003.
6 Ruth Little and Emily McLaughlin, *The Royal Court Theatre Inside Out* (London, 2007), p. 267.
7 Vincent O'Connell, 'The Play's the Thing', *Guardian*, 1 November 2003.
8 Peter Morris, 'The Brand of Kane', *Arete*, no. 4 (2000), 143–52.
9 Martin Crimp, 'Four Unwelcome Thoughts', in *Plays* 2 (London, 2005), p. xiii.
10 AS, pp. 4–10.
11 Mark Ravenhill, *Plays: 1* (London, 2000), p. 25.
12 Ken Urban, 'An Ethics of Catastrophe: The Theatre of Sarah Kane', *Performing Arts Journal*, no. 69 (2001), 36.
13 Aleks Sierz, 'In-Yer-Face Theatre: New British Drama Today',

Journal of English Teaching, vol. 9 (2002), 9.

14 John McRae and Ronald Carter, *Routledge Guide to Modern English Writing* (London, 2004), p. 41.

15 Elaine Aston, *Feminist Views on the English Stage: Women Playwrights, 1990–2000* (Cambridge, 2003), p. 80.

16 David Ian Rabey, *English Drama Since 1940* (Harlow, 2003), pp. 175, 206.

17 Clare McIntyre, *My Heart's a Suitcase and Low Level Panic* (London, 1994), pp. 3–4.

18 GS, p. 44. Claire McIntyre was also briefly Sarah Kane's tutor when she attended the MA playwriting course at Birmingham University.

19 Heidi Stephenson and Natasha Langridge, *Rage and Reason: Women Playwrights on Playwriting* (London, 1997), pp. 134–5.

20 Mary Luckhurst, 'An Embarrassment of Riches: Women Dramatists in 1990s Britain', in Bernhard Reitz and Mark Beninger (eds), *British Drama of the 1990s. Anglistik and Englischunterricht*, vol. 64 (Heidelberg, 2002), p. 73.

21 Dromgoole, *The Full Room*, p.162.

22 Clare Bayley, 'A Very Angry Young Woman', *Independent*, 23 January 1995.

23 GS, pp. 52–3.

24 David Edgar (ed.), *State of Play: Playwrights on Playwriting* (London, 1999), p. 17.

25 Jo Littler, 'Creative Accounting: Consumer Culture, the "Creative Economy" and the Cultural Policies of New Labour', in Timothy Bewes and Jeremy Gilbert (eds), *Cultural Capitalism: Politics After New Labour* (London, 2000), p. 217.

26 David Morley and Kevin Robins, 'The National Culture in its new Global Context', in David Morley and Kevin Robins (eds.), *British Cultural Studies* (Oxford, 2001), p. 9.

27 Brian Logan, 'The Savage Mark of Kane', *Independent on Sunday*, 1 April 2001.

28 Bob Vernon, '*Blasted*: A Savage Play Looks Beyond Indifference to a Savage World', *Guardian*, 23 January 1995.

29 Aleks Sierz, 'Planned Offensive', *The Stage*, 4 January 2001, p. 4.

30 Jack Tinker, 'This Disgusting Feast of Filth', *Daily Mail*, 19 January 1995.

31 Charles Spencer, 'Awful Shock', *Daily Telegraph*, 20 January 1995.

32 Phil Gibby, 'Here's to a Brave new Theatrical World', *The Stage*, 9 February 1995.

33 AS, p. 99.

34 Charles Spencer, 'Admirably Repulsive', *Daily Telegraph*, 5 April 2001.

35 GS, p.147.

36 Examples include Tony Harrison's *Phaedra Britannica* (1975) which sets the play in the context of the British Raj; Brian Friel's *Living Quarters* (1977) locates the play to Ireland and is subtitled 'After Hippolytus'; Timberlake Wertenbaker's *The Love of the Nightingale* (1988) uses the Hippolytus myth more as a secondary source to another Greek myth – that of Philomele, Procne and Tereus. The same territory is also explored in Joanna Laurens's play *The Three Birds* (2000).

37 Jeffrey Richards, Scott Wilson and Linda Woodhead (eds.), *Diana: The Making of a Media Saint* (London, 1999), p. 1.

38 Aleks Sierz, 'Review of the *Complete Plays*', p. 115.

39 Nils Tabert (ed.), 'Gespräch mit Sarah Kane', in *Playspotting: Die Londoner Theaterszene der 90er* (Reinbeck, 1998), p. 2.

40 Christopher Innes, *Modern British Drama 1890–2000* (Cambridge, 2002), p. 530.

41 AS, p. 183.

42 For further commentary see GS, pp. 90–1, 95–8.

43 Joe Hill-Gibbins, 'Notes from the Rehearsal Room', *Royal Court Young Writers Programme: Sarah Kane Resource Pack*, p. 18.

44 James Christopher, 'Rat with Hand Exits Stage Left', *Independent*, 4 May 1998.

45 James Macdonald, 'They Never Got Her', *Observer*, 28 February 1999.

46 For instance David Benedict commented, 'For better or worse, the spell of most plays drifts off the moment you leave the theatre. Not Sarah Kane's *Cleansed* . . . its compelling, horror-soaked atmosphere refuses to be shaken off', in 'Real Live Horror Show', *Independent*, 9 May 1998.

47 Georgina Brown, *Mail on Sunday*, 24 May 1998.

48 Ruby Cohn, 'Sarah Kane, An Architect of Drama', *Cycnos*, vol. 18, no. 1 (2001), 44.

49 Paul Taylor, *Independent*, 23 February 1999.

50 GS, pp. 130–1.

51 Peter Morris, 'The Brand of Kane', 150.

52 Alastair Macaulay, *Financial Times*, 8 May 1998.

53 Caridad Svich, 'What the Mirror Sees', *Hunter On-line Theater Review*; www.hotreview.org/articles/whatthemirror.htm.

54 Rachel Haliburton, 'Poetry of Despair', *Evening Standard*, 30 June 2000. The phrase 'suicide note' was mentioned directly in almost every review. A representative selection includes the following: Michael Billington, 'How Do You Judge a 75-Minute Suicide Note', *Guardian*, 30 June 2000; Paul Taylor, 'A Suicide Note That Is Extraordinarily Vital', *Independent*, 30 June 2000; Susannah Clapp, 'Blessed Are the Bleak', *Observer Review*, 2 July 2000.

55 See *RAM*, Netherlands Television (VPRO), broadcast 3 April 2005. The play's director James Macdonald also makes a similar point. See AS, p. 125.

CHAPTER 2

1   Mikhail Bulgakov (1891–1940). Russian prose writer and dramatist. Major novels include *The White Guard* (1925) and *The Master and Margarita* (1928–40); plays include *The Days of the Turbins* (1925–6) and *Flight* (1925–8).

2   For a fuller analysis of the relationship between the two plays see GS, pp. 95–6.

3   For a fuller analysis of the relationship between *Cleansed* and *The Ghost Sonata* see GS, pp. 94–5.

4   For a further discussion on the relationship between *Godot* and *Blasted* see GS, pp. 55–6.

5   In a later interview with Aleks Sierz (18 January 1999), Kane said, 'In retrospect I think the first third was influenced by Ibsen and Pinter, the middle section by Brecht and the final section by Beckett.'

6   For a discussion about Kane's attempts to adapt the play and its relationship to *Phaedra's Love* see GS, pp. 72–4, 77, 81.

7   Albert Camus (1913–60) was a French writer. *The Outsider* (1946) was one of his most well-known novels and bears some remarkable similarities with *Phaedra's Love* in terms of themes

and actual incidents such as the condemned Mersault meeting with a priest. For a fuller analysis see GS, pp. 73–4.

8 Bill Buford, *Among the Thugs* (1991). Kane's account of the incident is slightly inaccurate. Buford's story involves a football hooligan named Mark who stops at a Turkish restaurant to buy cigarettes. The restaurant is host to a private party held by the local CID. One of the officers fetches Mark a packet of cigarettes, but being known to him adds, 'You've got your fags. Now, hurry up you cunt and get the fuck out of here.' Mark vows revenge for the insult and tells fellow hooligan Harry about the incident who gatecrashes the party, assaults the officer and sucks/bites out his eye (p. 241). It is likely that Kane is mixing up her story about the police officer working undercover as a football hooligan from the film *I.D.* (1995), written by her friend Vincent O'Connell. Here, two police officers infiltrate a local 'firm', or gang of football hooligans to obtain intelligence, but slowly become drawn into their way of life.

9 The Dover scene in *King Lear* involves a meeting between estranged father Gloucester and his son Edgar. Gloucester has been blinded through torture and Edgar is disguised as a lunatic beggar. Gloucester asks the stranger if he will assist his suicide by leading him up to Dover cliff. Edmund appears to assist the request, but in fact thwarts it. In *Blasted*, Cate does the same by removing the bullets from the blinded Ian's gun. For more analysis of this scene see GS, pp. 59–60, and Graham Saunders, '"Out Vile Jelly": Sarah Kane's *Blasted* and Shakespeare's *King Lear*', *New Theatre Quarterly*, vol. 20, no. 1 (2004), 75–6.

10 Kane is alluding to the storm scene in *King Lear*. Here the monarch, after estranging himself from his three daughters, is homeless and faces the storm accompanied only by his Fool.

11 At the time of the interview *Cleansed* had not yet been completed and Kane envisioned it forming, together with *Blasted*, part of a trilogy about war. She later abandoned this idea.

12 Kane is referring to the 1996 Royal Shakespeare Company production directed by Sean Holmes.

13 To my knowledge, no documentary sources exist to support this statement.

14 T. S. Eliot, *The Frontiers of Criticism* (Minnesota, 1956), p. 11. For further commentary on the relationship between *Crave* and

The Wasteland see GS, pp. 102–5, 107–8; Eckart Voigts-Virchow, 'Sarah Kane, a Late Modernist: Intertextuality and Montage in the Broken Images of *Crave*', in Bernhard Reitz and Heiko Stahl (eds.), 'What Revels Are In Hand: Assessments of Contemporary Drama in English in Honour of Wolfgang Lippke', *CDE-Studies* 7 (Heidelberg, 2001), pp. 205–20.

15 *Victory* (1983) is set in the English Restoration. Bradshaw is the widow of one of the regicides who signed the death warrant of Charles II's father.

16 An alternative epithet given at the time to writers from Kane's generation before being superseded after 2001 by the more commonly used term 'in-yer-face' theatre.

17 The other play most critics attended was a production of August Strindberg's *The Dance of Death*. For further accounts of the press night see GS, pp. 94–5; AS, pp. 94–9.

18 To be fair to Michael Billington, while dismissive of *Blasted*, he did not question Kane's sanity. In the review that Kane does mention ('This Disgusting Feast of Filth', *Daily Mail*, 19 January 1995), Jack Tinker commented, 'Some will undoubtedly say the money [from the Jerwood Foundation which supports the Royal Court] might have been better spent on a course of remedial therapy.'

19 On 17 January 1995, the city of Kobe experienced the largest earthquake to hit Japan since 1923. More than 102,000 buildings were destroyed and more than 300,000 people were made homeless. Kane's reference to the rape and murder of a fifteen-year-old girl paraphrases a letter fellow playwright David Greig wrote to the *Guardian* in response to the treatment of *Blasted* by the press: 'On the same day when a fifteen-year-old girl was raped and murdered, both the tabloids and the *Guardian* felt it necessary to devote more space to attacking a young writer who has done nothing more than represent the abuse she sees in the world around her' in 'Truthful Exploration of Abuse', *Guardian*, 24 January 1995. It is likely that the story both Kane and Greig allude to is the conviction of Roger Connors, a support worker who raped (but did not murder) a fifteen-year-old girl. A further victim came forward and Connors was jailed for nine years on account of both rapes. See 'Support Worker Jailed for Rape', *Guardian*, 25 January 1995.

20 The story Ian dictates – 'A serial killer slaughtered British tourist
Samantha Scrace . . . ' (12) – seems to have been inspired by real-
life events concerning the 'Australian Backpacker Murders',
where between December 1989 and April 1992 two British
women, two Australians and three Germans were abducted after
hitchhiking and murdered. Their bodies were discovered in the
Belanglo State Forest, ninety miles south of Sydney. Ivan Miliat,
an unemployed labourer, was convicted and sentenced to life
imprisonment in 1996. Like Ian's account, the British tabloid
press privileged the murders of the young British victims rather
than the other nationalities, in an echo of Ian's description of the
murdered girl as a 'bubbly nineteen year old' (12). In one newspaper article (Robert Milliken, 'Hitch-Hike Murders Suspect to
Stand Trial', *Independent*, 13 December 1994), the mother of
one of the British victims, Joanne Clarke, described her daughter
as 'quite bright and bubbly'.

21 A form of epilepsy, where a temporary disturbance of brain
function is produced through abnormal electrical activity within
the brain itself. Characterised by a brief lack of self-conscious-
ness (commonly referred to as 'absence'), in which speech/motor
function is temporarily halted.

22 At one point after emerging from a fit Cate says, 'Have to tell her
. . . she's in danger' (9).

23 Andrea Dworkin (1946–2005). American feminist and writer,
most well known for her work that drew comparisons between
pornography, prostitution and male sexual violence. Books
include *Woman Hating* (1974) and *Pornography: Men Possessing
Women* (1981).

24 Kane's assertion that rape was not carried out by the North
Vietnamese forces seems to be true. In contrast, reports of
Vietnamese women being raped by American soldiers has been
substantiated. The most infamous incident was the My Lai
massacre, where on the morning of 16 March 1968 an American
patrol slaughtered the inhabitants of the village of My Lai in
Quang Ngai province. In the Bosnian conflict evidence exists
that the rape of Muslim women by Serbs was more of a general
policy than individual acts by soldiers. After the conflict, the
Bosnian government assembled details that revealed 13,000 rape
victims, although in 1993 the European Commission offered a

rough estimate of 20,000 women who had undergone systematic rape by Serbian soldiers. See Noel Malcolm, *Bosnia: A Short History* (London, 1994).

25 Caryl Churchill translated a version of Seneca's *Thyestes*, which was staged at the Royal Court's Theatre Upstairs in July 1994. The production was directed by James Macdonald.

26 Kane is referring to *The Alan Clark Diaries* (London, 1994).

27 Kane is referring to the fragment entitled '*Union*'. See Roland Barthes (trans. Richard Howard), *A Lover's Discourse: Fragments* (London, 1979), pp. 226–8.

28 Rick Rylance, *Roland Barthes* (Hertfordshire, 1994), p. 117.

29 Rick Rylance, *Roland Barthes* (Hertfordshire, 1994), p. 118.

30 Kane is talking about the fragment entitled 'Catastrophe'. Here, Barthes also expresses dismay at his own comparison, 'Is it not indecent to compare the situation of a love-sick subject to that of an inmate of Dachau? Can one of the most unimaginable insults of History be compared with a trivial, childish, sophisticated, obscure . . . comfortable subject'? However, Barthes concluded the two are synonymous, in that both share a terrible power whereby, 'I cannot recover myself, regain: I am lost forever'. See Barthes, *Lover's Discourse*, p. 49.

31 Mandela makes no mention of this person or incident in his autobiography *Long Walk to Freedom*, or any other source to my knowledge.

32 Play written and directed by German theatre/filmmaker Rainer Werner Fassbinder in 1969. Its structure is similar to *Crave*, where character is designated by letters. Six murder stories are recounted in the play, one featuring Moors murderers Ian Brady and Myra Hindley. For an analysis of Fassbinder's play see David Barnett, *Rainer Werner Fassbinder and the German Theatre* (Cambridge, 2005), pp. 101–8.

33 Aleister Crowley (1875–1947). Occultist and mystic who belonged to The Order of the Golden Dawn and practised Cabalistic magic. Crowley was also a diabolist who claimed to be the Beast from the Book of Revelation. In *Crave*, A quotes the central philosophy from Crowley's *Book of the Law*, 'Do what thou wilt shall be the whole of the law' (199).

34 The actor Andrew Maud appeared as Doctor/Priest/Theseus in the original Gate production of *Phaedra's Love* in 1996.

35 This example bears a close resemblance to an essay by Edward Bond entitled *Our Story*. Written in 1995, it was published in a collection of essays entitled *The Hidden Plot* (London, 2000), pp. 3–9. Although the volume was published after Kane's death, it is possible she may have been sent the article as Bond had previously included one of his poems, *Le Théâtre de la Cité* (1998), in a letter to her which was later included in the *Hidden Plot*. Bond himself was not certain whether he sent the piece to Kane, but pointed out that she may have got the idea from other work he had written [Letter to author, 26 December 2005].

36 Influential 'Indie' beat group of the mid 1980s, based around brothers Jim and William Reid. In turn, their audiences were renowned for their violent behaviour, often rioting after performances. The group broke up in 1999.

37 The show was entitled *Cabaret of Smiles* and has continued to tour internationally.

38 Nasa Theatre ('Nostalgic Actors and Singers Alliance') formed in 1989. On their tenth anniversary, the group renamed themselves *Siya* ('Only Move'). The company employ traditional music, dance and drama within the context of modern Zimbabwean life.

39 Mona Hatoum (b. 1952). Palestinian-born artist whose work encompasses performance, video, sculpture and installation work. The work Kane refers to is entitled *Deep Throat* (1996) in which a table is laid out for a meal. However, the plate is actually a screen on which is projected the video of an endoscopic voyage through the artist's body.

40 John Peter, 'Alive and Kicking', *Sunday Times*, 29 January 1995.

41 Not strictly true. Kane did write for television, but none of the scripts was made into actual programmes. See GS, pp. 150–1.

42 Dennis Potter (1935–94). Playwright best known for his work on television, including *Pennies from Heaven* (1978), *Blue Remembered Hills* (1979) and *The Singing Detective* (1986).

43 Not strictly true. The film was first broadcast on British television at 11.35 p.m.

44 Alan Clarke (1935–90). Influential film and television director, whose most innovative work has been for television. Clarke is usually associated with dramatists who seek to expose injustice within marginalised and demonised communities. Work for

television includes David Rudkin's *Penda's Fen* (1974), David Leland's *Made in Britain* (1983) and Al Hunter's *The Firm* (1989). Films include *Scum* (1977), *Billy the Kid and the Green Baize Vampire* (1985) and a film adaptation of Andrea Dunbar's play *Rita, Sue and Bob Too* (1986).

45 *Ashes to Ashes* opened at the Royal Court (temporarily located at the Ambassadors Theatre), London on 12 September 1996.

46 Georges Bataille (1897–1962). French essayist, theorist and novelist. Sex, death and the practical application of the obscene were recurring themes in his work. Like Artaud, Bataille was associated for a time with the Surrealist movement.

47 Franca Rame (b. 1929). Italian actress and playwright. Married to dramatist Dario Fo, with whom she has frequently collaborated. The play is in the form of a monologue by a woman describing the ordeal of being gang raped. The play Kane refers to has two English versions. The one most readily available is Franca Rame and Dario Fo, *A Woman Alone and Other Plays* (London, 1991). Here, it is called *The Rape*. The other edition uses the title Kane refers to: *Dario Fo and Franca Rame, Theatre Workshops at the Riverside Studios London* (London, 1983). Kane's unpublished *Comic Monologue*, which she wrote before *Blasted*, also takes as its subject a young woman who has been raped by her boyfriend.

48 Russian writers and composers had been subject to censorship and denunciation when the 1934 Soviet Writers' Congress declared that literature would follow an ideological agenda based around social realism and associated work that would privilege patriotic themes and the concerns of workers. Experimental 'modernist' writing and music were denounced as symptomatic of bourgeois western values. After Stalin's death in 1953, a limited degree of artistic liberalisation followed.

49 This version of the play is contained in *Frontline Intelligence: New Plays for the Nineties* (London, 1994).

50 In interview Macdonald commented, 'The rain between the scenes may have come partly from looking at photographs of Bosnia at the time, because as you know much of the play is rooted in that conflict. I can remember saying to Sarah, "Listen, we're going to need some kind of sound to get from A to B to C, and cover us running around in the dark". And she said, "I'm

not having bloody theatre music in my play"! So then the onus was on me to come up with something!' GS, p. 122.

51 These changes made their way into a subsequent edition published by Methuen in 1996, which also includes *Phaedra's Love*.

52 Samuel Johnson (1709–84). Critic, lexicographer and poet. Johnson dismissed the blinding of Gloucester as 'an act too horrid to be endured in dramatic exhibition, and such as must always compel the mind to relieve its distress by incredulity'. See Walter Raleigh (ed.), *Johnson on Shakespeare* (Oxford, 1959), p. 160.

53 No Renaissance play exists to my knowledge with such a stage direction. It is possible that Kane might be thinking of the anonymous medieval morality play *Everyman* (c.1520) which contains the stage direction, '*An* Angel *appears in a high place with Everyman's Book of Reckoning, and receives the soul, which has risen from the grave.*' See G. A. Lester (ed.), *Three Late Medieval Morality Plays* (London, 1999), p. 101.

54 *The Winter's Tale* (c.1610–11) includes one of Shakespeare's most celebrated stage directions, '*exit pursued by a bear*' (III.iii 57).

55 It is likely that Kane is referring to Judy Upton's *Ashes and Sand* which is set in a southern British seaside town and concerns a teenage girl gang. The play, which premiered in December 1994, immediately preceded *Blasted* at the Royal Court's Theatre Upstairs.

56 Play by John Arden (b. 1930). Premiered at the Royal Court in 1959. Philip Roberts concurred with Kane, 'It was almost universally attacked in the notices, and almost universally regarded by the artists as an extraordinary work. It took 25 per cent at the box office'. See Philip Roberts, *The Royal Court and the Modern Stage* (Cambridge, 1999), p. 73.

57 Kane is referring to *Real Classy Affair* (1998). Grosso's previous works – *Peaches* (1994) and *Sweetheart* (1996) – adopted a form based loosely around the conventions of social realism.

58 Not strictly true. Kane finished the course, but because of her refusal to pay a compulsory sanatorium fee the degree was not awarded. Kane refused to pay because she saw the fee as effectively being a private health care levy. Following *Blasted*, she was eventually allowed to graduate, although the fee was never paid.

59 Howard Barker visited the University of Birmingham after Kane left. On 13 March 1995, he gave a public lecture entitled, 'The Glass Confessional: the Theatre in Hyper-Democratic Society'. He also spoke separately to students on the MA Playwriting course.

60 See 'Author's Note: On Violence', in *Plays: One* (London, 1991), pp. 9–17; and 'Author's Preface' to *Lear* in *Plays: Two* (London, 1983), pp. 3–12.

61 Kane is referring here to an infamous scene in Quentin Tarantino's film *Reservoir Dogs* (1992) where a police officer is tortured and murdered. During the scene, his ear is severed with a razor to the song 'Stuck in the Middle With You' by Stealers Wheel that is playing on the wireless throughout the torture scene.

62 Criminal Justice and Public Order Act 1994. Introduced by John Major's Conservative government. The Act made a number of amendments to the existing law. Kane drew attention to areas that placed restrictions on existing rights and increased penalties for categories of perceived antisocial behaviour. These included changes to a suspect's right to silence, increased police rights to stop and search and also take/retain bodily samples. Perhaps in response to the prominence the media had given to illegal 'rave' parties, the Act specifically included sections against collective trespass on land that had previously been civil offences.

63 Manchester beat group formed in 1977. They recorded two albums *Unknown Pleasures* (1979) and *Closer* (1980). The band's lead singer Ian Curtis hanged himself on 18 May 1980. The line in *4.48 Psychosis* 'The chicken's still dancing/the chicken won't stop' (243) is an allusion to Werner Herzog's film *Stroszek* (1977), which singer Ian Curtis is thought to have watched shortly before his suicide. The line 'The chicken won't stop' was inscribed into the end groove of the gramophone record *Still* (1981), which contained posthumously released material from the band. See Deborah Curtis, *Touching from a Distance: Ian Curtis and Joy Division* (London, 1995), pp. 128–9.

64 Artistic director of the Royal Court, 1992–8.

65 Performed at the Donmar Warehouse, London, in 1987.

CHAPTER 3

1   The British production also had an American actress, Madeleine Potter, although she adopted a British accent in performance.

2   Mark Swed, '*4.48 Psychosis* Gives Life to Sarah Kane's Final Suicide Gasp', *Los Angeles Times*, 6 November 2004.

3   In the original production, the cast looked at many of the books Kane was reading at the time of her death. These included the following: C. S. Lewis, *The Silver Chair*; Albert Camus, *The Myth Of Sisyphus*; Sylvia Plath, *The Bell Jar*; Edwin S. Schneidman, *The Suicidal Mind*; Lewis Wolpert, *Malignant Sadness: The Anatomy of Depression*; Elizabeth Wurtzel, *Prozac Nation: Young and Depressed in America: A Memoir*.

4   Max Stafford-Clark was artistic director of the Royal Court 1981–93. Stephen Daldry, his successor, commented on the fertile working relationship during the hand-over period: 'Max educated me in lots of ways . . . the age gap was a huge advantage because Max could take me on as a pupil in a sense.' Cited in Roberts, *The Royal Court Theatre and the Modern Stage* (Cambridge, 1999), p. 219.

5   *Death and the Maiden* premiered at the Theatre Upstairs in July 1991 and transferred to the main stage in November where it ran until December that year. The production transferred to the Duke of York's Theatre in February 1992 where it ran until November. *Oleanna* was performed at the Theatre Downstairs from January until August 1993. It transferred to the Duke of York's Theatre in September until June 1994. Max Stafford-Clark maintained that a £300,000 surplus had been built up during this period. Cited in Roberts, *The Royal Court Theatre and the Modern Stage* (Cambridge, 1999), p. 219.

6   The temporary move took place in 1996 and the Royal Court reopened in February 2000.

7   See Graham Saunders, '"Just a Word on the Page and There Is the Drama": Sarah Kane's Theatrical Legacy', *Contemporary Theatre Review*, vol. 13, no. 1 (2003), 99–101.

8   Sarah Kane Symposium, FIND (5th Festival of International New Drama), Schaubühne am Lehniner Platz Theatre, Berlin, 19 March 2005.

9   Literary manager of the Royal Court Theatre.

10 See Dromgoole, *The Full Room*, p.162.

11 Samuel Beckett, *The Complete Dramatic Works* (London, 1990), p. 119.

12 'It's like that when I touch myself . . . Just before I'm wondering what it'll be like, and just after I'm thinking about the next one, but just as it happens it's lovely, I don't think of nothing else' (22–3).

13 See also Aleks Sierz, *The Theatre of Martin Crimp* (London, 2006), p. 67.

14 Sierz is perhaps being unfair here. Simon Block has had a succession of plays produced since the 1990s in both London and New York. These include *Place at the Table* (2000), *Hand in Hand* (2002) and *Everything is Illuminated* (2006). Block is also a successful writer for British television on series such as *Trust* (2000), *New Tricks* (2004) and *The Inspector Lynley Mysteries* (2005). Richard Zajdlic has also in recent years moved into television, writing for the long-running soap opera *Eastenders* as well as series such as *Attachments* (2000) and *Clocking Off* (2000). While it is true that Rebecca Prichard has not had work produced for the stage recently, in 2003 she wrote the screenplay for the film *Butterfly World*.

15 See Ken Urban, 'The Body's Cruel Joke', in Nadine Holdsworth and Mary Luckhurst (eds), *A Concise Companion to Contemporary British and Irish Drama* (Oxford, 2007), pp. 152–67.

16 See GS, pp. 160–1.

17 See AS, p. 108.

18 Samuel Beckett's stage directions describe the figure in the following way, '*tall standing figure, sex indeterminable, enveloped from head to foot in loose black djellaba, with hood, fully faintly lit, standing on invisible podium about 4 feet high . . . dead still throughout but for four brief movements where indicated*', *Complete Plays*, p. 376.

19 Letter to the *Guardian*, 23 January 1995.

20 J. B. Priestley, *An Inspector Calls* (London, 1965), p. 65.

21 David Edgar's *Playing with Fire* (2005) was a response to the interracial riots. The following year Channel 4 screened a drama-documentary, *The Bradford Riots*, based on some of the events that took place.

22 The Author's Note to *Blasted* says, 'Stage directions in brackets

( ) function as lines' (p. 2). Simon Kane, who manages his sister's literary estate, commented that these instructions 'do not mean that it was Sarah's intention that they be used as dialogue. It means that they are distinct actions that occur at the precisely specified place in the dialogue and should be completed without overlapping dialogue from the following speakers. Of course it may be perfectly valid to speak stage directions, but that's a production decision, not something that the text encourages'. E-mail to the author, 4 January 2006.

23 American actor and dramatist. *Killer Joe* was playing in the West End at the same time as *Blasted*. Kane's debut was unfavourably compared to Letts by several critics. For a discussion of the play see GS, p. 11; AS, pp. 53–6.

24 The Christian Democratic Union of Germany (CDU) under Chancellor Helmut Kohl were in power from 1982 to 1998.

25 Marius von Mayenburg. An English translation by Maja Zade of his 1997 play *Feuergesicht* (*Fireface*) premiered at the Royal Court in May 2000, where several critics drew comparisons to the early work of Sarah Kane.

26 Mel Kenyon is alluding to the 1994 season of plays by new writers, staged at the Royal Court Theatre Upstairs.

Select Bibliography with Annotations

A – Primary Material

Works by Sarah Kane

Comic Monologue (1991); *Starved* (1992); *What She Said*
  (1992). The three monologues were known under the
  collective title of *Sick*. Although unpublished, copies
  are held at the University of Bristol Theatre Collection.
  Viewing is by appointment only. For details, visit
  www.bris.ac.uk/theatrecollection. The collection also
  contains materials relating to Kane's performance in a
  student production of Howard Barker's *Victory* and her
  direction of Shakespeare's *Macbeth*.

Blasted. This version of the play is contained in *Frontline*
  Intelligence: New Plays for the Nineties (London, 1994).
  Selected and introduced by Pamela Edwardes.

Blasted and *Phaedra's Love* (London, 1996). In this edition
  Sarah Kane makes several small but significant changes to
  Blasted.

Skin (ten-minute film).

Cleansed (London, 1998).

Crave (London, 1998).

4.48 Psychosis (London, 2000).

Sarah Kane: Complete Plays. Introduction by David Greig
  (London, 2001). This edition also contains the script of
  Skin. All of the plays in this volume, with the exception of
  4.48 Psychosis, underwent minor revisions by Kane shortly
  before her death.

Newspaper Articles

'The Only Thing I Remember is', *Guardian*, 13 August 1998.
  Diary style article written during the Edinburgh Festival in
  which Kane lists memorable and formative theatrical and
  non-theatrical 'performances'.

'Drama with Balls', *Guardian*, 20 August 1998. Diary style
  article written during the Edinburgh Festival. Kane writes
  of her frustrations about theatre when placed against other
  performative arts – notably football; discusses rehearsal
  process for *Crave*.

B – Secondary Sources

Critical Studies

BOOKS

Iball, Helen, *Sarah Kane's Blasted* (London, 2008). Insightful
  exploration of Sarah Kane's debut play.

Saunders, Graham, *'Love Me or Kill Me': Sarah Kane and the
  Theatre of Extremes* (Manchester, 2002). Introductory
  study that looks at major themes running through Kane's
  work and chapters on each play; appendix contains interview material relevant to Kane's drama.

PARTS OF BOOKS AND EDITED COLLECTIONS

Aston, Elaine, *Feminist Views on the English Stage: Women
  Playwrights, 1990–2000* (Cambridge, 2003), pp. 77–97.
  Chapter on Kane with perceptive readings of *Blasted*,
  Cleansed and *Crave*; argues that oppositional gender
  relations underpin the plays; contains chapters on work of
  other new female dramatists' from the 1990s; also evaluates
  older dramatists work during the decade.

Brannigan, John, *Orwell to the Present: Literature in
  England, 1945–2000* (London, 2003), pp. 136–161.
  Locates Kane within the canon of post-war British theatre
  and read through a tradition of trauma, beginning with
  Osborne's *Look Back in Anger*, Bond's *Saved* and

Ravenhill's *Shopping and Fucking*.

Buse, Peter, *Drama and Theory: Critical Approaches to Modern British Drama* (Manchester, 2001), pp. 172–190. Chapter on *Blasted* read through trauma theory.

Innes, Christopher, *Modern British Drama 1890–2000* (Cambridge, 2002), pp. 528–36. Brief but thoughtful assessment of Kane's work.

Little, Ruth, and McLaughlin, Emily, *The Royal Court Theatre Inside Out* (London, 2007). Discussion of *Blasted* and *Cleansed*, including new interview material with those who worked with Kane.

Luckhurst, Mary, 'Infamy and Dying Young: Sarah Kane, 1971–1999', in Luckhurst, Mary and Moody, Jane (eds), *Theatre and Celebrity in Britain 1660–2000* (London, 2005), pp. 107–26. Examines changing nature of Kane's 'celebrity'; examines early association with sensation and inclusion within brand of 'Cool Britannia' to iconographic status following suicide.

McRae, John and Carter, Ronald, *Routledge Guide to Modern English Writing* (London, 2004), pp. 37–41. Brief assessment of Kane's work; locates her as a key figure in British post-war drama.

Parry, Philip, 'Sarah Kane (1971–1999)', in Jay Parini (ed. and intro.), *British Writers: Supplement VIII* (New York, 2003), pp. 147–61. Overview and assessment of Kane's work.

Rabey, David Ian, *English Drama Since 1940* (London, 2003), pp. 191–208. Perceptive chapter on new dramatists in the 1990s; includes section that provides closely argued overview of Kane's work.

Sierz, Aleks, *In-yer-face Theatre: British Drama Today* (London, 2001), pp. 90–121. Influential first study of new British dramatists in the mid 1990s; contains a chapter on Sarah Kane.

Stephenson, Heidi and Langridge, Natasha, *Rage and Reason: Women Playwrights on Playwriting* (London, 1997). One of the first major interviews with Sarah Kane.

Urban, Ken, '"The Body's Cruel Joke": The Comic Theatre of
Sarah Kane', in Holdsworth, Nadine and Luckhurst, Mary
(eds), *A Concise Companion to Contemporary British and
Irish Drama* (Oxford, 2007), pp. 152–67. Thoughtful
examination of Kane's use of comedy.

Waters, Steve, 'Sarah Kane: From Terror to Trauma', in Mary
Luckhurst (ed.), *A Companion to Modern British and Irish
Drama* (Oxford, 2006), pp. 371–82. Looks at the reception
of Kane's work.

ARTICLES

Carney, Sean, 'The Tragedy of History in Sarah Kane's
Blasted', *Theatre Survey*, vol. 46, no. 2 (2005), 275–96.
Makes a comparison between *Blasted*, Bond's *Saved* and
Brenton's *The Romans in Britain* in terms of their reception
and depiction of violence.

Farrier, Stephen, 'Approaching Performance through Praxis',
Studies in Theatre and Performance, vol. 25, no. 2 (2005),
129–43. Examines relationship between theory through
practice with *Crave* as one practical example for exploring
Judith Butler's theories of identity and performativity.

Gottlieb, Vera, 'Theatre Today – the "New Realism"',
Contemporary Theatre Review, vol. 13, no. 1 (2003), 5–14.
Examines 1990s British culture; argues that Kane and other
'in-yer-face' dramatists lacked political focus.

Iball, Helen, 'Room Service: En Suite on the *Blasted*
Frontline', *Contemporary Theatre Review*, vol. 15, no. 3
(2005), 320–9. Questions the rapid canonisation of *Blasted*
and analyses the *mise en scene* of its hotel setting.

Morris, Peter, 'The Brand of Kane', *Arete*, vol. 4, (2000),
143–52. Provocative assessment of Kane's posthumous
reputation.

Nikcevic, Sanja, 'British Brutalism, the "New European
Drama", and the Role of the Director', *New Theatre
Quarterly*, vol. 20, no. 3 (2005), 255–72. Examines
negative impact of recent embrace of British playwrights in

Europe; hostile and factually incorrect readings of Kane's and Ravenhill's work.

Rebellato, Dan, 'Sarah Kane: An Appreciation', *New Theatre Quarterly*, vol. 15, no. 3 (1999), 280–1. Personal tribute and assessment of Kane's work; argues that after *Cleansed* there is a move from violence to an examination of love, albeit against a background of cruelty and despair.

Saunders, Graham, '"Just a Word on the Page and there is the Drama": Sarah Kane's Theatrical Legacy', *Contemporary Theatre Review*, vol. 13, no. 1 (2003), 97–110. Assesses critical reaction to Kane's work since her death.

—, '"Out Vile Jelly": Sarah Kane's *Blasted* and Shakespeare's *King Lear*', *New Theatre Quarterly*, vol. 20, no. 1 (2004), 69–77. Comparative reading of *Blasted* in relation to Shakespeare's *King Lear*.

Sierz, Aleks, 'Sarah Kane Checklist', *New Theatre Quarterly*, vol. 17, no. 3 (2001), 285–90.

Singer, Annabelle, 'Don't Want to Be This: The Elusive Sarah Kane', *The Drama Review*, vol. 48, no. 2 (2004), 139–71. Gives a reading of the plays against a background of Kane's depression and suicide.

Solga, Kim, '*Blasted*'s Hysteria: Rape, Realism, and the Thresholds of the Visible', *Modern Drama*, vol. 50, no. 3 (2007), 347–73. Well-argued reading, based on the implications behind the invisibility of Cate's rape in *Blasted*, both as a staged act, and in critical responses to the play.

Urban, Ken, 'An Ethics of Catastrophe: The Theatre of Sarah Kane', *Performing Arts Journal*, no. 69 (2001), 36–69. Discusses 2001 Sarah Kane season at the Royal Court; argues that Kane's drama is based on ethics that emerge from catastrophic events, yet fails to offer solutions or catharsis to an audience; traces origins of 'in-yer-face' drama and its break from a socialist playwriting tradition to one predicated on Howard Barker's theoretical writings for a 'Theatre of Catastrophe'.

Urban, Ken, 'Towards a Theory of Cruel Britannia: Coolness, Cruelty, and the 'Nineties', *New Theatre Quarterly*, vol. 20, no. 4 (2004), 354–72. Wide-ranging and thoughtful account of 'Cool Britannia' and the new theatre writing associated with the period; argues that Kane and her con-temporaries eschewed the cynicism and distance of their contemporaries in Britart and instead presented audiences with an
enervating theatre of cruelty.

Wixon, Christopher, '"In Better Places": Space, Identity, and Alienation in Sarah Kane's *Blasted*', *Comparative Drama*, vol. 39 (2005), 75–91. Thoughtful reading of *Blasted* which looks at the various uses Kane makes of stage space in the play.

NEWSPAPER ARTICLES

Reviews of specific plays have been excluded unless otherwise stated, as have pieces that do not contribute to a fresh assessment of Kane's work.

Armitstead, Claire, 'No Pain, no Kane', *Guardian*, 29 April 1998. Includes interview with Kane in which she discusses *Cleansed* and talks about the developments her work has taken in *Crave*.

Benedict, David, 'Real Live Horror Show', *Independent*, 9 May 1998. Detailed review of *Cleansed* that attempts to analyse its complex theatrical imagery.

___, 'The Taboo Shaker', *Evening Standard*, 30 March 2001. Interview with James Macdonald, who discusses the season of Kane's work at the Royal Court.

Christopher, James, 'Rat with Hand Exits Stage Left', *Independent*, 4 May 1998. Reviews *Cleansed* and includes an interview with James Macdonald who discusses its theatricality and the European sensibility of Kane's work.

Fanshawe, Simon, 'Given to Extremes', *Sunday Times*, 26 April 1998. Discusses the innovative staging used for the

Royal Court production of *Cleansed*; includes interview material with James Macdonald, Jeremy Herbert and Ian Rickson.

Farr, David, 'Walking into her Rehearsal was like Entering a Religion', *Daily Telegraph*, 26 October 2005. Personal account by David Farr on the circumstances that led him to commission *Phaedra's Love*.

Greig, David, 'Truthful Exploration of Abuse', *Guardian*, 24 January 1995. Letter from the playwright defending *Blasted*.

Hattenstone, Simon, 'A Sad Hurrah', *Guardian Weekend*, 1 July 2000. Feature article on Kane's work to coincide with the premiere of *4.48 Psychosis*; discusses Kane's work and includes personal reminiscences from friends and colleagues.

Logan, Brian, 'The Savage Mark of Kane', *Independent on Sunday*, 1 April 2001. Assessment of Kane's legacy in response to the 2001 Royal Court season of plays; includes interviews with Ian Rickson and James Macdonald.

Macdonald, James, 'They Never Got Her', *Observer Review*, 28 February 1999. Includes a personal tribute to Sarah Kane and brief assessment of her importance as a dramatist prepared to use new theatrical forms.

Mahoney, John, '*Blasted* Theory', *Guardian*, 23 October 2003. Sees Kane and her contemporaries having a detrimental influence on continental playwriting.

Nightingale, Benedict, 'Passion that Still Blazes', *The Times*, 3 April 2001. Retrospective piece on Kane in light of the 2001 Royal Court season devoted to her work.

Ravenhill, Mark, 'Suicide art? She's better than that', *Guardian*, 12 October 2005. Personal assessment of Kane's posthumous reputation.

——, 'The Beauty of Brutality', *Guardian*, 28 October 2006. Account and assessment of Kane's career mixed with personal anecdotes.

Sierz, Aleks, 'The Filth, the Fury and the Shocking Truth', *The Times*, 24 October 2005. Retrospective article written in response to the 2005 British revivals of *Phaedra's Love* and *Cleansed*; includes interview material from Simon Kane, Anne Tipton and Sean Holmes.

Swed, Mark, '4.48 *Psychosis* gives life to Sarah Kane's final Suicide Gasp', *Los Angeles Times*, 6 November 2004. Review of the Royal Court's 2004 American touring production of 4.48 *Psychosis*.

INTERNET SOURCES

Numerous sites make mention of Kane's work. However, the selection below is chosen on the basis of their in-depth treatment of her work or ongoing scholarly interest.

4.48 *Psychosis Theatre Programme*; www.calperfs.berkeley.edu. Programme for the Royal Court's 2004 production of 4.48 *Psychosis* which toured America.

Aberg, Maria, Young Genius: *Phaedra's Love*; www.youngvic.org. Educational resource pack produced for the 2005 Young Vic/Barbican *Young Genius* series of plays; pack includes timeline dating from Kane's birth to death, including significant political and cultural events; interview with Anne Tipton, director of *Phaedra's Love*; and design pictures of the production.

Graeae; www.graeae.org. Information on the company's 2006 production of *Blasted*; documentation includes director's comments on the play, actor's diaries, a photo gallery and an education pack to download.

In-Yer-Face-Theatre; www.inyerface-theatre.com. Site maintained by Aleks Sierz; contains sections devoted to Sarah Kane and her contemporaries.

Literary encyclopaedia; www.litencyc.com. Entries on all five of Kane's plays and *Skin*; contributors Graham Saunders, Aleks Sierz and Julie Waddington.

New York Theatre Experience; www.nytheatre.com/
nytheatre/voiceweb/v_urban.htm. Interview with
playwright and academic Ken Urban, who discusses
Kane's work and the American premiere of *Cleansed*.

Sarah Kane; www.iainfisher.com/kane.html. Site dedicated
to Kane's work; contains an archive, links, photographs
and a discussion forum.

Svich, Caridad, 'What the Mirror Sees';
www.hotreview.org/articles/whatthemirror.htm.
Review of the 2004 Royal Court American tour of
4.48 Psychosis.

Theatrevoice; www.theatrevoice.com. Includes audio
recordings of the following: interview with Matt Peover,
who directed the 2004 production of *Crave* at Battersea
Arts Centre; post-show discussion of Oxford Stage
Company's 2005 production of *Cleansed* with a panel
including Dominic Dromgoole, Sean Holmes, Simon Kane,
Graham Saunders and Aleks Sierz.

GENERAL SOURCES

Barker, Howard, *Arguments for a Theatre* (Manchester,
3rd edn 1999).

Barnett, David, *Rainer Werner Fassbinder and the German
Theatre* (Cambridge, 2005).

Barthes, Roland (trans. Richard Howard), *A Lover's
Discourse: Fragments* (London, 1979).

Bewes, Timothy and Gilbert, Jeremy (eds), *Cultural
Capitalism: Politics After New Labour* (London,
2000).

Bradwell, Mike (ed.), *The Bush Theatre Book: Frontline
Drama 5* (London, 1997).

Buford, Bill, *Among the Thugs* (London, 1992).

Glenny, Misha, *The Fall of Yugoslavia: The Third Balkan War*
(London, rev. edn 1993).

Lampe, John, *Yugoslavia As History: Twice There Was a
Country* (Cambridge, 2nd edn 2000).

Malcolm, Noel, *Bosnia: A Short History* (London, 1994).
Raleigh, W. (ed.), *Johnson on Shakespeare* (Oxford, 1959).
Rylance, Rick, *Roland Barthes* (Hertfordshire, 1994).

Acknowledgements

I would like to thank the following for their help in the preparation of this book: Mark Batty; Edward Bond; Amanda Bull; James Christopher; Frances Babbage; Lia Ghilardi; David Greig; Chris Lee; Philip Roberts; Sarah Shaw; Nils Tabert; Robert Wilcher (to whom I owe so much); Resham Naqvi, Elizabeth Tyerman and Dinah Wood at Faber. Simon Kane corrected and clarified factual information.

I would also like to thank the interviewees Jo McInnes, Ian Rickson, Aleks Sierz (who also helped on all manner of Kaneology-related queries), and Jeremy Weller.

For permission to reprint copyright material, the publishers gratefully acknowledge the following:
CLAIRE ARMITSTEAD: 'No Pain, No Kane', reproduced by kind permission of the *Guardian*; CLARE BAYLEY: 'A Very Angry Young Woman', reproduced by kind permission of the *Independent*; DAVID BENEDICT: 'What Sarah Did Next', reproduced by kind permission of the *Independent*; SARAH KANE: 'The Only Thing I Remember Is' and 'Drama with Balls', reproduced by kind permission of the *Guardian*; ANDREW MCKINNON (ed.): 'Interview with Sarah Kane and Vicky Featherstone', reproduced by kind permission of the editor; NATASHA LANGRIDGE and HEIDI STEPHENSON: *Rage and Reason: Women Playwrights on Playwriting*, reproduced by permission of Methuen Publishing Ltd; BENEDICT NIGHTINGALE: 'Disgusting Violence? Actually it's Quite a Peaceful Play', reproduced by kind permission of the *Independent on Sunday*; NILS TABERT: 'Gespräch mit Sarah Kane', *Die Londoner Theaterszene der 90er*, reproduced by permission of the author.

Index